HOPE ELIZABETH POWERS

JOURNEY
TO THE
BEGINNING

Escaping Domestic Violence and Living to Tell My Story

LIFEWISE BOOKS

JOURNEY TO THE BEGINNING

Escaping Domestic Violence and Living to Tell My Story

BY HOPE ELIZABETH POWERS

Unless otherwise noted, all scriptures are taken from the THE MESSAGE: THE BIBLE IN CONTEMPORARY ENGLISH (TM): Scripture taken from THE MESSAGE: THE BIBLE IN CONTEMPORARY ENGLISH, copyright©1993, 1994, 1995, 1996, 2000, 2001, 2002. Used by permission of NavPress Publishing Group

Scriptures marked NIV are taken from the NEW INTERNATIONAL VERSION (NIV): Scripture taken from THE HOLY BIBLE, NEW INTERNATIONAL VERSION ®. Copyright© 1973, 1978, 1984, 2011 by Biblica, Inc.™. Used by permission of Zondervan

Scriptures marked ESV are taken from the THE HOLY BIBLE, ENGLISH STANDARD VERSION (ESV): Scriptures taken from THE HOLY BIBLE, ENGLISH STANDARD VERSION ® Copyright© 2001 by Crossway, a publishing ministry of Good News Publishers. Used by permission.

Published by:

⛭ LIFEWISE BOOKS

PO BOX 1072
Pinehurst, TX 77362
LifeWiseBooks.com

hopepowers.com

ISBN Print: 978-1-952247-96-5
ISBN Ebook: 978-1-952247-97-2

DISCLAIMER

For safety concerns and to maintain anonymity, the names of all individuals have been changed in this book, as well as identifying characteristics and details such as physical properties, occupations, and places of residence. Locations of events have also been changed, but the events described in this book actually happened. The author did her best to share the details exactly as they occurred according to her memory.

CONTENTS

"Oh, thank God—he's so good!
His love never runs out.
All of you set free by God, tell the world!
Tell how he freed you from oppression."

PSALM 107:1-2

TELL YOUR STORY

"Tell your story." These words are like a sword that pierces my soul. We all have a story. A story of good, bad, ugly, or perhaps even redemption. "Tell your story"—such a simple three-word request but profoundly difficult. These were the words the district attorney spoke to me after enduring a terror that was unimaginable. My story involves the demonic, unspeakable acts of horror, violence, abuse, and darkness. The kind of darkness that is completely void of light. The kind of darkness that was so consuming it sought to take out my light and life. Yet through the darkness, a light began to shine. A perfect light that cast out all darkness. This light is hope, and this hope can only be found in Jesus Christ our Lord and Savior.

> "The Life-Light blazed out of the darkness;
> the darkness couldn't put it out."
>
> JOHN 1:5

Even though this part of my life seems to have concluded, I feel like it is just beginning. Often, I wish I could return to certain points and do things differently. Most of us would probably like a "do-over" in some part of our life, but my do-over would stretch almost thirty years. I can relate to the Bible story of Jonah and how God told him to go to Nineveh, but instead, he fled and went the other direction toward Tarshish and ended up in the belly of the large fish. After several days, Jonah was returned to where he started in Joppa.

> "Next, God spoke to Jonah a second time: 'Up on your feet and on your way to the big city of Nineveh! Preach to them. They're in a bad way and I can't ignore it any longer.' This time Jonah started off straight for Nineveh, obeying God's orders to the letter."
>
> JONAH 3:1-3

Why would anyone go to Nineveh? It was a bad place to be. I know for me, I would rather stay in my comfort zone, like Jonah, and go somewhere safe. But it seemed to me that the Lord was saying to Jonah after his disobedience, "Let us try this again, Jonah. Go to Nineveh, in spite of your fears." The second time, Jonah obeyed God and went to Nineveh, as this was a much better option than being in the belly of a fish. Just when life feels comfortable, we may receive the call to go to our version of Nineveh and try to resist because we think we know better.

How many times did I think to myself, if only I could get a second chance to return to Joppa and start over, without ending up in the belly of a fish, where it is an even more hopeless situation? Lord, I will go to Nineveh now. Please give me a do-over. Where or what is your Nineveh? Did you end up taking a wrong turn, not following God, and end up somewhere worse? It is not too late to listen. The Lord has promised, "I'll make up for the years of the locust, the great locust devastation—locusts savage, locusts deadly, fierce locusts, locusts of doom, that great locust invasion I sent your way." (Joel 2:25) Our God is truly one of second chances (and third, fourth, fifth and on). His love and mercy are boundless.

> "GOD's loyal love couldn't have run out, his merciful love couldn't have dried up. They're created new every morning. How great your faithfulness!"
>
> LAMENTATIONS 3:22-23

It has been several years, but I still struggle with all the events that took place during this time in my life. It has taken me a long time to come to the place where I could write down my experiences. When I have tried to write in the past, I have come under attack from the enemy, but I am determined to fulfill God's purpose for my life before I run out of time because this message is urgent. I often think of the urgency in the Bible story of Esther, who was placed in a position to save God's chosen people. Not because she wanted this responsibility nor even because she asked for it, but because God chose her to fulfill His sovereign promise to Israel. Although I am no Esther, I am certain I must complete this task God has set before me.

For the longest time, I saw my story and the aftermath as a curse I had incurred, but now I see my circumstances as an opportunity to share Jesus Christ's redemption with others. I believe the Lord has and will continue to bless me so that my story may be a blessing to others who face domestic violence or abuse.

I tell my story not because I want to share this horror, but because I want to tell of God's redemption. I believe it is God's purpose for my life—to tell my story so that others may find hope in a hopeless situation. I am broken, anxious, often afraid, and certainly do not deserve God's grace. However, as Paul spoke of Christ's grace and mercy regarding his handicap, I know my weakness and limitations can be used as a gift as His power is made perfect in my weakness.

"'My grace is enough; it's all you need. My strength comes into its own in your weakness.' Once I heard that, I was glad to let it happen. I quit focusing on the handicap and began appreciating the gift. It was a case of Christ's strength moving in on my weakness. Now I take limitations in stride, and with good cheer, these limitations that cut me down to size—abuse, accidents, opposition, bad breaks. I just let Christ take over! And so the weaker I get, the stronger I become."

2 CORINTHIANS 12:9-10

THE SEVEN TRUTHS

There are seven truths I experienced regarding domestic violence that I want you to clearly see as I tell my story. First, and most importantly, domestic violence can happen to anyone. There is no demographic, age, ethnicity, gender, or religious affiliation it cannot touch. Domestic violence is an equal opportunity offender. This crime is not confined to the poor or marginalized in society, although this is what we often hear. Domestic violence does not exclude those who may be wealthy, highly educated, or an executive of a company.

According to statistics provided by the National Coalition Against Domestic Violence (NCADV) in 2018, one in three women and one in four men have experienced some form of physical violence by an intimate partner. This includes a range of behaviors such as slapping, shoving, and pushing. One in four women and one in seven men have been victims of severe physical violence, such as beating, burning, and strangling by an intimate partner in their lifetime. Seventy-two percent of all murder-suicides involve an intimate partner, and ninety-four percent of the victims in these crimes are women.[1] I am certain these statistics may have increased with the onset of the global pandemic in 2020. Nonetheless, these are staggering numbers that communicate that domestic violence likely touches every family, even those in the church.

Second, it is important to know the warning signs or "red flags" of behavior that may be a precursor to domestic violence, even if the signs are subtle. Once you see the signs, get out of the relationship and do not look back. Get help! I cannot emphasize this enough. I know you may be in love with the potential abuser, but God never intended for you to live a life of abuse and imprisonment. Trust me, the situation will NOT get better. With God on your side, you are stronger than you think.

Third, do not buy into the lie that marriage or other relational commitments, such as living together, having a child, or engagement, will make it better. Often abusers will tell their victims that if only they would marry them, they will no longer be possessive or jealous (the potential cause of their actions). They are convincing, but it is a lie. The abuse will get worse, not better. Think of this, if your abuser is on his or her best behavior when you are dating, imagine how they will be when you are married and they no longer have to keep up the act because now, they have you. You are trapped.

Fourth, Jesus is calling us into freedom. He is calling us into a new life free from the guilt and shame of abuse. We are not called to live our life as a prisoner under the rule and authority of an abuser. This is not the life God wants us to live. This is the reason Jesus died on the cross. Burn that bridge, start a new life, and do not look back. We all deserve better.

The fifth important truth I want you to see is that people and relationships can be toxic and evil. Although Jesus specifically tells us to love our neighbor, we are not required to be around toxic or abusive people, even if they are believers. A friend once told me that as much as God hates divorce, He loves you that much more. God does not want us to be around someone who is abusive, either verbally, emotionally, spiritually, or physically, even if we are married to them. This is not how God designed relationships. Walk away from toxic people and relationships if they cannot or refuse to be reconciled.

Sixth, God sees you right in your circumstances and has a plan for your life—"plans to take care of you, not abandon you, plans to give you the future you hope for." (Jeremiah 29:11). While it might be difficult to start over financially or emotionally, there are people and places that can help you. Reach out for help and always ask God for guidance.

> "Trust GOD from the bottom of your heart; don't try to figure out everything on your own. Listen for GOD's voice in everything you do, everywhere you go; he's the one who will keep you on track."
>
> PROVERBS 3:5-6

Last but not at all least, there is healing and life after domestic violence. Domestic violence does not have to be a lifelong sentence. No matter what you have done in your past, you do not deserve to be in an abusive relationship. Maybe no one will know about your situation or maybe everyone will know. But either way, the opinions of others do not matter. Statistically speaking, many of those who point fingers have experienced or are experiencing what you had the courage to walk away from. Keep in mind, Jesus was rejected repeatedly. One of Jesus's closest companions was Mary Magdalene, who was cleansed of seven demons (Luke 8:2), so she was deeply engaged in the dark side. The Samaritan woman at the well was the first person who Jesus "publicly" trusted to identify himself as the Messiah. In a quiet one-on-one conversation with her, He revealed to her all she had done. Not as a judgement but in love (John 4).

Why do you think Jesus would choose to identify with the marginalized people in society? As described in Mark 2:17, "Jesus, overhearing, shot back, 'Who needs a doctor: the healthy or the sick? I'm here inviting the sin-sick, not the spiritually-fit.'" Jesus was also rejected by His own people and peers. I know that I qualify in both sin and rejection. So do not be disheartened when others mock you or look down on you. Hold your head high because you have been redeemed and can identify with Jesus. Hallelujah!

As I mentioned earlier, my goal in telling my story is not to relive the nightmares I have experienced over the last several years but to trust in God's purpose and providence in my life. We, as Christians, are called to advance HIS Kingdom, but perhaps my purpose and calling may be guided in telling my story. To those who are still suffering under the hands of an abuser, I pray my story gives you hope and courage. To those who are abusers, I pray my words will echo in your heart and lead you to a place where you too can find repentance and healing through Jesus Christ. Abuse of any kind should never be part of a loving relationship. There is healing through the Savior.

As I follow God's commandment to tell my story, my prayer is that the Lord will be magnified through it, as He was the key player in getting me back to the beginning.

CHAPTER 1

THE INTOXICATING POISON

"A hostile world! I call to God, I cry to God to help me. From his palace he hears my call; my cry brings me right into his presence—a private audience!"
Psalm 18:6

REFLECTIONS IN THE MIRROR

At almost fifty years old, I sat by the mirror combing my long blonde hair getting ready to meet someone who might be the love of my life. As I glanced in the mirror at my reflection, I lamented over the difficulty in my life. Love had been cruel and harsh, yet I had never given up hope. Perhaps I was naïve and still lived in the Cinderella fantasy world where Prince Charming would one day ride in and swoop me off my feet. This fantasy is known as the Cinderella syndrome.[2]

As I glanced deeper at my reflection, the years spoke their truth. I could not figure out where the time had gone with not much to show for it. I could not believe I was almost fifty years old. For almost twenty-five years, I was married to an abusive alcoholic. I had managed to raise three children, and once the youngest was about to graduate from college, I had to get out of the marriage as I could no longer take the drinking and resulting abuse.

The screaming and yelling all the time was the worst. I had a relentless ringing in my ears for years from all the screaming and yelling my ex-husband dished out to me. I would cower under his accusations. His rants could go on for hours, and I would hope and pray that the evening would end with him passing out and not another vicious assault. I would often wonder how he could continue living with the amount of alcohol he consumed and why the Lord would not intervene and just strike him dead with a heart attack or other alcohol related ailment. This deathwish was wrong, and I knew it. So I would repent but continued to feel terrible guilt for these feelings. Then, I would pray for my death as I saw it as the only way out. Maybe he would kill me or I would just die. But then what about my children? Where would my death leave them? It was endless misery.

During these years, I suffered terrible bouts of anorexia, along with anxiety and depression. Thinking back, anorexia was more of a means to an end for me than a body image issue. Anorexia was definitely a control issue. Nothing in my life was in control. I was totally controlled. But I soon found I could control food. I know it sounds crazy, but when you have reached a point in your life where you have no freedom and are controlled or so it seems, you tend to do things that can only make sense to someone who has walked down the same path. I was a Christian, and I did pray to God, but it seemed like He was silent as I continued to endure this nightmare. I know God heard my prayers of desparation, but I couldn't understand why my situation never changed. I had to get out. I could no longer take it after enduring this abuse for more than half of my life.

During all those years, I did everything I could to protect and shield my children from the abuse. I pretended we had a happy, normal family, living in a happy, normal home. But in the end, this was a lie. When I finally left the relationship, I was accused of all kinds of indecencies and sins that were not true by my soon-to-be ex-husband. He intentionally turned my children against me. To this day, I still struggle in the relationship with one of my children, who somehow never forgave me for all of the things they were told I did. I pray God will fully restore this relationship, as my oldest child saw the abuse I endured firsthand and how often I protected them against this. I pray every day for the softening of their heart as I can see progress, and I have faith that one day this relationship will be fully restored.

Somehow, I was able to get an education during my tumultuous first marriage. Early on, I realized I would need to have a way to provide for my children. During my years in college, it was difficult to maintain my grades as my husband would demand my attention and then go on with his rants until the wee hours of the morning. There were times I did not sleep for days due to his rants and then trying to complete my studies. Despite the difficulties, I managed to graduate and get a good job. Over the years, I had been able to have a stable and successful career, despite the situation I lived in. I was even able to start my own business on the side, once I was free from the abuse of my first husband. My business was my passion, and it provided great joy to me as a ministry to help others.

Although I had success in my career and my side business, my life felt empty now without someone to share it with. I was alone for almost six years and lacked nothing but love and companionship. I had friends but that was different than having someone to share your life. Many of my friends were married so that was a bit awkward going out with them all the time, and the friends that were single only cared about finding a man. Surely, there had to be something in between.

In addition, my three children had completed college and were starting to see success in their careers and marriages. By this point, I had several grandchildren. Since I married very young and was used to always having my kids around, being alone was difficult and very uncomfortable for me. It made it feel like all these accomplishments I would normally celebrate meant nothing because I had no one to share them with.

I had failed relationship after failed relationship and could not seem to find the right person. *But maybe tonight would be the night*, I thought, as I combed my long blonde hair and looked positively at my reflection in the mirror again. *Maybe tonight would be different*, I thought. I have prayed about this one, and God has answered my prayer. He is the one. I can feel it.

> "Those who hear and don't act are like those who glance in the mirror, walk away, and two minutes later have no idea who they are, what they look like."
>
> JAMES 1:23-24

Eighteen months after my last failed relationship, I gave up on dating altogether. Under advice and counsel from a spiritual leader at my church, I focused on learning to be a good wife so that when Mr. Right came along, I would be ready. I gave my petition to God as to what I wanted in a mate and prayed diligently that he was out there somewhere and God, in His infinite providence, could arrange for us to meet. But after eighteen months of these prayers, it seemed hopeless. I was growing increasingly impatient. Maybe God was waiting on me to make a move? Maybe I needed to take a step of faith? Yes, this must be the delay. But how and where?

The singles group at church was no good. It was mostly women, and even though I enjoyed the company, it seemed like an unspoken catfight if a new man entered the group. The guys would usually visit once and then never return. I cannot blame them as the meetings were an invisible, intense battle of raging emotions and hormones (often not good ones). On one occasion, I was even chastised by some of the women in the singles group for not being on dating sites. I was told that I was being disobedient to God by not having a man as we were not made to be alone. I momentarily had a flashback to the advice I received twenty years ago from a pastor, who told me that regardless of the abuse, I should be a submissive wife. I was in the wrong, and therefore, my husband had the right to take the upper hand in the relationship, even if it meant abuse. Wow, can you believe a pastor told me this? Of course, all of this made me feel even more isolated and alone.

Plus, I had already decided that if a man was my age and single, there was probably a good reason. What I needed was a man who was widowed. Someone who truly knew how to have a relationship and love and care for someone but had lost his wife and was wanting to spend his last years with someone who was adventurous, exciting, and loved living life with him. So I created my wish list to God, "Send me a man who is a widower, no kids under eighteen, financially self-sufficient, and crazy about me." This was my prayer.

So now that I knew what I wanted, I just needed to know where I could find him. A friend of mine told me I should try an exclusive online dating service, and I immediately flashed back to my conversation at the singles group a few months back, where I was chastised for not being on a dating site. My friend was a bit older than me and was someone whom I trusted. She had used this service recently and described some of the quality dates she recently had. Even though I was skeptical, I thought, *why not?* She did say it was exclusive and cost a hefty price to join. If it worked for her, why would it not work for me? What could it hurt? All I would be out was money, right?

THE PURSUIT

I summoned all my courage and gathered information on the relationship website my friend told me about. By this point, I thought I was an expert at discerning any "fakes" and could weed through and find the perfect person. Looking back, I was a bit self-deceived. The site my friend directed me to made claims of marriage and romance for all who participated in their discretionary services, of course with a hefty price tag. I trusted this site would be a safe option as the cost seemed prohibitive. Plus, my friend recommended it to me. I joined and worked on creating the perfect profile to attract the perfect mate. I continued to pray to God regarding this match, after all, I had given Him my "want" list for my next husband, so I was certain God would send me what I wanted because I was stepping out in faith and taking action.

After several dates, the site certainly did not live up to my expectations. Most of the men were not what I had prayed for or expected. They lied on their profiles. I decided to give up on this option. I needed to focus on an upcoming work conference and did not have time for this nonsense dating site.

The conference I had planned was five, almost twelve-hour days in a row. Most of the talks were in a language I did not understand. Even though there was a translator, it was brutal, as people argued for hours over who should have access to reports and other mindless information. While this torture was going on, a match popped up on the dating site. Someone wanted to connect with me.

Honestly, I would have never replied if I had not been so bored at this conference. My norm was to not reply right away to anyone who messaged me from the site as I did not want to appear anxious or desperate. But boredom took over, and I replied back. Then he replied back, and so it began. I agreed to receive text messages from him as he seemed nice, and he was everything I had prayed for. Could this be the man I had been waiting for? Was this last minute match an answer to my prayers?

INTERJECTION ON PRAYER

I interrupt my story for an interjection on prayer.

Over the last few years, I have longed to get closer to God by walking in the center of His will and being able to discern His voice. Through all my trials and tribulations, I have concluded that prayer is the key because it is the communication method God established. I certainly do not consider myself an expert on prayer, and there are a number of great books that explain prayer in more detail than I ever could, but I can speak to my experience and how my prayers were heard by God.

He sent answers to me along the way and even numerous red flags, which I ignored. I was fooled into believing I was hearing God's voice by Satan, the great deciever. Friends, the enemy is out there waiting for the precise moment to pounce on our weakness. For me, he knew exactly when and where to strike for the final kill and to destroy me for good.

But God had other plans for me. Now, I pray with confidence and know God listens and hears me. He is my protector from the evil one.

> "And if we're confident that he's listening, we know that what we've asked for is as good as ours."
>
> 1 JOHN 5:15

Have you ever had an experience that caused your hair to stand up on the back of your neck? You saw or heard something that caused this sensation, or it happened for no discernable reason, but you know beyond a shadow of a doubt something was amiss and not right. Some people would call this a gut feeling or a sixth sense, but I like to think this is God's way of prompting me to take heed and listen to His still, small voice. I can't count how many times I ignored His prompting because it was about my agenda, not His. This turned out to be a catastrophic mistake for me.

> "Rip the cover off those frauds and see how attractive they look in the light of Christ. Wake up from your sleep, climb out of your coffins; Christ will show you the light! So, watch your step. Use your head. Make the most of every chance you get. These are desperate times!"
>
> EPHESIANS 5:13-16

Now, back to my story.

RED FLAGS

It all started as a simple text conversation with a man I will call Joe. At this time, Joe and I had not had an actual verbal conversation, yet we were getting to know each other. He texted me pictures of his fancy cars and some of his purchases on a shopping trip and asked me what I thought. It was a bit strange how he was bragging about these things this way. I dismissed it thinking I should not be making snap judgements of someone who I had never even had a verbal conversation with. What if I mistake his display as something he didn't intend it to be?

In one of our text conversations, I mentioned my passion for exercise and how I worked out regularly. I was involved with all types of exercises including kickboxing, high intensity training, and dance. I also ran long distance. For most men, my level of fitness could be intimidating as I could run circles around most people my age. However, Joe did not miss a beat and displayed no intimidation whatsoever. *Great*, I thought to myself, *someone who has self-esteem and would not be intimidated by a woman who could outrun him*. But then the conversation went downhill quickly.

The subject turned to the kickboxing classes. I was not ever a fighter, then or now, but I did enjoy kickboxing and training like a boxer as a means of cardiovascular exercise. The kickboxing (and related violence to this sport) immediately perked Joe's attention. As I jokingly texted and laughed that I was sure I could take him (in a race), Joe's demeanor turned toward the fighting aspect of kickboxing, and he challenged me to a match. As I continued to make jokes about running, Joe's comments became darker regarding the ensuant battle he longed for, so much so that it made the hair on the back of my neck stand up (red flag).

At that moment, I had the overwhelming feeling to never reply and block Joe's number. Besides, Joe knew nothing about me but my name and general area of location where I lived. Against better judgment, I collected myself and thought, what can you gather from text messages anyway? It is difficult to discern the full meaning behind text messages. Right? Finally, I broke his incessant tirade by texting that "I am a lover not a fighter."

How many times do I wish I could have returned to that moment and listened to that still, small voice of the Lord trying to warn me of the impending danger I was about to face! I mentioned this quandary to a few of my friends, and they agreed that it is sometimes difficult to discern meaning from a text. They encouraged me to have an actual conversation before I made my mind up on him. This sounded right, so I decided we should have a verbal conversation before I made any judgements. I agreed to take a call from Joe later that week. We talked for hours. He seemed like the perfect man. After that night, we talked every day for hours, until we finally agreed to meet for our first date.

THE FIRST MEETING

Finally, after two weeks of talking and texting, Joe and I had our first date. We decided to go out for dinner and drinks just to chat and get to know each other better. The plan was for Joe to pick me up at my apartment and then we go to dinner at a nice restaurant close by my home. (By the way, a word of caution, you should never let someone know where you live on a first date, especially someone you have never met. Meet them at a public location and have an exit plan.)

I was very excited to meet Joe as he was exactly what I requested from the Lord. Joe was widowed, and his only child, a daughter, was in her twenties and married. Best of all, Joe was financially independent. Joe looked strikingly handsome in his Armani suit, expensive jewelry, and fancy sports car as he arrived to pick me up. I will say I was impressed as I stood on my balcony to watch when he arrived. Joe had that bad boy look perfected!

The date went off without a hitch. I was charmed and mesmorized all at once. I felt like Cinderella with Prince Charming. We talked for hours late into the night. I did not want him to leave or the night to end. It was truly magical. There he was—the man of my dreams—after all these years. I was breathless. All thoughts of red flags vanished.

GOING DOWN THE RABBIT HOLE

After the first date, we continued talking every night for hours, sometimes until the early morning. Joe was charming, attentive, and considerate. I did ask Joe briefly about the weird text conversation from the beginning, and he laughed it off saying he was joking around and wanted to see how I reacted. If I had taken him up on his offer to fight it would have been a red flag to him. Nothing was ever said about it again, and I completely wrote it off as a misunderstanding.

When I inquired about Joe's job, he told me he was retired. *Wow—retired in his fifties*, I thought to myself. Amazing. Joe said he was formerly an executive, and his company was taken over by another company. He was given a generous severance plus he had received a substantial amount of money upon his wife's death from her life insurance policy. He also told me he received a huge inheritance when she passed away, along with the inheritance he received when his parents passed. He told me he had enough money to live like a king until he was one hundred years old, so why continue to work? How could I argue with that point? I did check out the story Joe told me about his former employer, and yes, the company was taken over as he described. Sadly, I never questioned his employment with the company or his status as an executive.

Joe's wife died about one year prior to our meeting. I inquired if this was a bit too early for him to be seeking a relationship. He confirmed that he had loved his wife dearly, and although she had been seriously ill throughout the twenty-year marriage, her death was rather unexpected. While he grieved for her every day, Joe felt he must move forward with his life now. He told me that his wife would have wanted him to find someone who would make him happy so he would not spend years of his life grieving her loss. He assured me he had gone to grief counseling and several months into our relationship even took me to meet his counselor at his last session. Joe told the counselor at the meeting that he had met another love and that there was room in his heart to love again.

Soon after our first date, Joe inquired if I would ever be upset if he surprised me by showing up at my home with flowers or a gift when I was not expecting it. *Of course not, who would be upset about getting this attention?* I thought. One evening when I had finished working late, I called Joe but he did not answer. This was unusual so I texted him that I had tried to call and was headed to the grocery store to pick up some food for dinner. I drove to the grocery store which was only a block from my home and parked and entered the store. Since it was later in the evening, only one entrance was open.

As I entered, I heard baskets clanging and people talking and laughing loudly. There was Joe in the middle of it, trying to hide so I would not see him. I was shocked. He quickly grabbed my elbow and told me to come with him to his car. It was quite strange and unexpected but in the front seat of his car was a large bouquet of flowers. He explained that he was waiting on me to get home from work and was going to surprise me. Since I was running late, he had to go for a pit stop and could not wait any longer. He decided to go into the nearest grocery store to use the facilities and received my text while he was inside. He did his best to avoid me in the grocery store, but since there was only one exit available, he ran right into me as I entered.

I quickly completed my grocery shopping, and he followed me to my home, where we laughed and laughed about the incident. I could tell I was falling head over heels for Joe, and he felt the same about me. After the grocery store incident, Joe and I became inseparable. Life with Joe was like a never-ending carnival. He accompanied me almost everywhere I went, and we laughed and had so much fun together.

Joe said he could not stand to be apart from me. I wanted to be with him too. Joe joined all my exercise classes, even the dance classes and charmed his way into the group of girls who always attended. Joe quickly became a regular and everyone seemed to adore him. Joe even went with me to the nail and hair salon and got to know all the regulars there also. He laughed and said he was starting to feel like one of the girls. I told him he must be mad! And he agreed that he was madly in love with me. I felt the same about him.

As Easter approached, I wanted Joe to go to church with me. He admitted to me that he was angry with God for taking his wife, but he knew she was in heaven. They attended church when she was able, and they were both saved. Since he had met me though, Joe confided that he thought of me as his savior. I laughed and suggested that maybe his "so-called" savior could help restore his relationship with the real Savior, Jesus Christ. Joe laughed and said yes, yes, yes! We attended a wonderful Easter service, and I felt so happy, especially to have Joe by my side. I told him how I had prayed so long for him and was so happy God answered my prayer. He smiled and agreed. It felt so perfect as if God had put us together. I never dreamed I could have been so happy.

FLY AWAY WITH ME

Before I met Joe, I planned a trip to the mountains with my best friend, Mary, and her husband, Dan. I often traveled with them as I did not like to travel alone, and they were happy to have me tag along. Mary and Dan were very laid back, and I could choose to do as little or as much with them as I preferred. They did not get their feelings hurt if I decided to go to listen to music or shop rather than hang out at the hot tub. I loved that about them.

I invited Joe to come, and he immediately accepted. He asked for my flight information, and by the time I got home from work that day, he had a ticket seated right next to mine for the vacation.

"How did you pull this off?" I asked.

Joe replied, "I have my ways, doll."

I called the resort and got his stay situated so he could share my room with me. We were all set. I told him I planned to arrive a few days prior to meeting Mary and Dan, so it would be a great time to relax and enjoy each other before doing some hiking and other excursions.

Joe was so excited. He had never been on a trip to the mountains or even traveled more than fifty miles from his home before due to his wife's illness and inability to be far from her doctors. He always dreamed of traveling but that was just it, a dream. Soon, we would be flying off to a new adventure.

WINED AND DINED

As the days rolled on and the relationship blossomed, Joe continued to be charming and debonair. He was extremely charismatic and sophisticated and seemed to adore me. Joe put me on a pedestal and worshiped the ground I walked on. At this point, we had only been dating a few weeks but had already become inseparable.

On the Saturday prior to our departure, Joe told me he had a big surprise for me. I reminded him I needed to go to the mall to pick up a few things, and he told me he was taking me to a very special place he was certain I had never been. I could not imagine where Joe was going to take me. I was excited beyond belief and ready to go. Before we could leave, Joe told me to wait as he had another surpise for me. What? Another surprise? Wasn't this trip to this new secret place surprise enough? Joe went into the bedroom and came out with a small wrapped box.

"Open it," he insisted and smiled.

I quickly opened the box and there was the most beautiful hair tie I had ever seen. It was a designer hair tie and must have cost him a small fortune.

"Put it on and let's go," he pleaded as we ran out the door to his convertible.

The car ride in Joe's convertible was so amazing. The weather was perfect, and Joe drove the long way around the city with numerous twists and turns so I could not figure out where we were going. I felt like Elizabeth Taylor in the movie, *A Place in the Sun*, driving down the interstate in his convertible with my hair tied back. Everything he did made me feel so special. No one had ever made me feel this special. No one had ever taken the time to truly show me how much they cared for me even down to the point of getting this beautiful tie to hold my long blonde hair back from the wind on the convertible ride.

Once we arrived at our destination, I could not believe my eyes. It was our local high end mall full of designer stores. Of course I had never

JOURNEY TO THE BEGINNING

been there because I certainly could not afford to buy anything. Joe knew all the employees in every store, and they called him by name. He introduced me as his new true love. I was on cloud nine. Nothing was off limits for purchasing and he insisted on buying me beautiful things that I could never afford for myself.

While I did not like such indulgence, I was mesmerized by the way he moved and eloquently described each item we viewed. I seemed to truly hurt his feelings when I would not accept his generosity of so many gifts. There was something inside of me that could not accept the gifts even as he was insistant I did. Something seemed over the top and extravagant about this. He assured me it was only because he had not been able to lavish his previous wife with gifts as she had recently died, and he wanted to show me how much he cared. Giving me these things was important to him. I certainly could and did provide for myself but not at this level. Joe thought I was worthy of the finest things in life or so he said. Again, I refer back to the Cinderella syndrome.

Following the designer mall trip, he took me to an exclusive and very expensive restaurant. We wined and dined for hours as we relished each other's company. Nothing could have made this surprise more special to me. I knew I had found my perfect man, and I praised God He sent someone so kind, generous, and loving to me. Little did I know that this fairy tale was to be very short lived. I didn't see then the manipulation and control I was setting myself up for by accepting Joe's gifts.

FAMILY TIES

Just prior to our vacation, I introduced Joe to my daughter, Rachel, and her husband. Rachel had three small children, so she was always busy and running after one or two of the kids. Rachel was impressed with Joe as he bounced the youngest of my grandchildren on his knee.

"Mom, you have hit the jackpot for a boyfriend," she said.

I told her I could not believe it. How long had I waited for him? It seemed like forever but now he was finally here.

"Have you told Joshua yet?" Rachel asked.

"Yes, I have told him. We are planning to go see Joshua soon so he can meet Joe," I said.

Joshua lived in St. Louis with his wife. Joshua was my baby and Rachel was in the middle. My oldest son, Caleb, lived on the other side of town with his wife and three children.

"Have you introduced Joe to Caleb?" Rachel asked.

"Soon," I replied.

Joe piped in, "I want to meet Caleb and Joshua, but your mom said you were her favorite so I had to meet you first."

Rachel smiled and laughed, "My mom did not say that."

I told Rachel we would meet Caleb when we returned from our trip and then plan a visit to see Joshua. Caleb was a little more reserved than Rachel or Joshua, so I was not sure how he would relate to Joe. Joe told me not to worry because he could charm anyone.

HE WOULDN'T TAKE NO FOR AN ANSWER

Joe seemed to be head over heels in love with me, and he did not want to wait to get married.

"Joe," I would say,"you might not really like me when you get to know me," jokingly as we had only known each other a few weeks at this point.

"How can you marry someone you have only known for a short time?" I asked him.

"Well, when its right you know it in your heart," Joe replied.

Joe confided to me that he had really been lonely since his wife passed away, and although she had been ill all those years prior, it was hard to be alone. I understood this all too well.

"Let's just live in the moment for now," I said, "and we can worry about tomorrow when it gets here."

Joe would smile and say, "Okay Hope, but I *will* marry you."

I smiled and knew that one day we would get married but not too soon. I wanted to make sure he was truly the one.

LIMITLESS BARRIERS

It was finally time for our vacation together. We already had such an amazing time just being in each other's company. How could this situation get any better? I was so lucky to have found a man that was crazy about me and loved me for who I was in spite of all my faults. Only God could have sent someone so wonderful, I thought.

We met up with Mary and Dan a few days after we arrived at the mountain resort. This was the first time they had met Joe, and they immediately liked him. Mary and Dan were very skeptical of my previous dates and were a little protective of me since they had witnessed me struggle so much in my first marriage. I was a little nervous at their reaction, but when Mary pulled me aside to tell me that I hit the jackpot and they could tell that Joe was crazy about me, I was relieved. Plus, Rachel said the same thing. As the vacation commenced, the magic continued for Joe and I.

This is not to say there wasn't any conflict. Joe was still somewhat obsessed with his now deceased wife. He routinely commented how she would have loved to travel and have these types of adventures if only her health would have allowed. He would often cry in reflection of these memories. At first, I was sympathetic and responded in a way as to provide him with love and affection. I wanted him to know he could have new experiences that would not replace his wife but allow her memory to reside in the appropriate location in his mind. This constant obsession with his deceased wife was truly a foreshadowing of events to come. Unfortunately, I could not see it at the time, but it was another red flag.

Soon my sympathy wore thin, and I finally became upset with his constant lamenting. While I may sound somewhat insensitive, that was not the case at all. Joe was so fixated on her memory he could not live in the present. One night while in deep discussion about his deceased wife, Joe and I went out on our hotel room balcony to watch the stars. He became violently angry and threw his wine glass over the balcony. He wept bitterly, and while his violence was not targeted at me, I know now it was another sign of the lawlessness, unpredictability, and erratic rage this man could exhibit. Following this incident, Joe seemed to be calm and no longer mourned her. I thought maybe this whole display was just part of the grieving process and these moments would come and go. I never told anyone about this incident.

During our ventures into nearby towns, Joe was insistent on purchasing an engagement ring for me, even though we had only known each other a short time. He was insistent that we should get married right away, but I did my best to slow things down. I was not convinced he was ready to move forward, given the grief he still felt. My best friend, Mary, was a little concerned over Joe's eagerness to get married. I told her not to worry. He may be eager, but I was going to take the actual engagement slow. She smiled and agreed.

We looked at every store for the perfect ring until finally we found it. The ring had to be set and sized, but the jeweler was very happy to do this before we departed the location. The ring contained a diamond over three carrots and was exquisite. Joe did not accept anything less than perfect. He was always spending huge amounts of money, and this ring seemed like a drop in the bucket for him. He told me he wanted me to have the best and make all of the other women jealous because I was married to someone so generous and loving. I believed that this fantasy could come true for me, one day.

While in the towns near our resort, there were numerous opportunities to spend money. There were outdoor markets, jewelry exhibits, shopping venues, and art galleries galore. I enjoyed visiting these types of places and looking at all the exquisite items. In the past, I bought some faux jewelry and replica paintings but nothing extravagant. Joe was immediately drawn into the shopping world in these towns, and everything I said I liked, he bought, spending over $100,000.00 during our time there.

Although I would tell him I did not want something, he would sneak back to purchase items to surprise me with when I would momentarily excuse myself to the ladies room or turn my head for a moment. I was shocked and kept telling him that just because I liked something did not mean I wanted it. I am not sure if this message ever became clear to him as he spent money like it was going out of style. I was not used to this extravagance, and it continued making me very uncomfortable. When I discussed my discomfort with Joe, he became very distraught and took this as a personal rejection. Over and over, I insisted that I was not rejecting him. I was not used to this elaborate spending. Joe reminded me of the lifetime of luxury that he intended to bestow on me. This did not seem real. How could this last? I knew in my heart this was too good to be true.

YOU ARE MINE

Soon enough, our dream vacation was over, and we had to go back to reality. Our life together was just starting, according to Joe, and we would have years of memories to make ahead of us. I agreed, and we quickly settled into a routine when we returned home. My workplace was not too far from my home, so I would go to work, and Joe would do errands or go and check on his daughter and home while I was at work. Joe used to tease me that I was such a slob, so he would insist that he must clean up after me. I was nowhere near as messy as Joe made me out to be, and I felt a little uncomfortable that he would go through my belongings when I was not home, but as he said, he was just organizing things so we would have more room—more room for his belongings.

Every day, Joe made me breakfast to take to work. The breakfast consisted of a protein shake and coffee. He even went so far as to set out my morning vitamins so I would not forget to take them. He preferred that I drink the protein shake and coffee with him before I left for work, but I was always running late. So he would pack them for me to take with me as long as I promised to drink them.

"Yes, dear," I would say, as I whisked out of the apartment.

Most days, Joe would pick me up from work, and we would go to lunch and spend the hour together. Every evening, we would go to one of the exercise classes or go for a run, followed by a nice dinner at one of his favorite restaurants in the area. Joe would always order wine with dinner, and we would share a bottle or sometimes two daily. I repeatedly told him I could not continue this lifestyle as I was not used to this much food and wine. I was starting to gain some weight. Joe insisted that I was too thin for his taste when he met me, so he felt it was his job to fatten me up.

"Don't worry," he would say. "You are the most beautiful woman in the world to me."

I still felt uncomfortable, so Joe started cooking dinners at home for me. He would make elaborate dinners and serve them with wine everyday. It was really no different than going out to eat as far as caloric intake went. Joe insisted that this option was better than going out every night as we could be alone and dine in candlelight. He was such a romantic. It was hard to resist his charm.

"You are mine, my beautiful Hope!" Joe would say. "Mine, all mine."

By this time, I truly was under his spell.

A SUDDEN DESCENT

"Joe?" I called to him early one Saturday morning.

Joe was already up milling around in the kitchen but immediately came into the bedroom.

"What is it love?" he answered.

"I have terrible pain in my legs, and I cannot move to get out of bed."

"What?" Joe answered, "Are you sore from the workout?"

"No," I replied, "this is different."

Joe immediately ran over to me in the bed and tried to lift me up. I cried out in pain. Everytime I moved my legs, a severe pain shot through my body. The pain was so intense that it brought tears to my eyes.

"Hang on, doll," Joe said, "Let me get you some ibuprofen as I am sure you must have strained a muscle or something."

Joe ran into the kitchen and returned with the ibuprofen and a glass of water.

"Here you go," he said, in a kind voice. "Take this and lay back down for a few minutes. I am sure this will help and the pain will subside."

Just as Joe had promised, the pain subsided in about twenty minutes, and I was able to get up and move again. Joe thought it must have been a strain from the previous day's workout, so he said we should take a day or two to rest just to make sure I did not aggravate the injury. I agreed, and the pain did not return again. Joe teased me that I was getting a little older, so maybe I should take it easier on my workouts. I laughed at that, but something was definitely amiss with the pain in my legs, but it had passed, and we moved on with our weekend plans as if nothing had happened.

UNEXPECTED DANGER

While the pain in my legs subsided, I began to notice pain in my arms. Just a little at first, but over time, I began to not be able to lift my arms above my shoulders. *This is strange*, I thought but kept this to myself. Several weeks after the incident with my legs, I was having trouble getting dressed for work. I found it difficult to slip my blouse over my head due to the pain in my arms. The pain was intense when I tried to lift my arms. Joe noticed I was wincing with pain and asked me what was wrong.

"Oh nothing," I replied, "just a little stiff from sleeping."

"Do you need some ibuprofen?" he asked.

"No, I am fine, thanks love," I said, as Joe handed me my protein shake and coffee as I walked out the door to go to work.

"Drink that protein shake," Joe commented as he kissed me goodbye for the day, "it will help with your stiffness."

As the stiffness and pain in my arms grew almost daily, I did my best to hide the pain from Joe. I did not want him to think something was wrong with me. I had been so vibrant and active when we met, and I wanted to stay that way, so we could spend the rest of our lives enjoying each other and going on adventures. Soon the pain and inability for me to lift my arms grew more severe. I could no longer hide it from Joe or others. I told Joe that maybe all the "bad" food from going out to eat and too much wine was to blame as I had never in my life gone on such a wild eating and drinking craze before. I always had eaten healthy and maintained a reasonable weight, but after weeks and weeks of this indulgence, my body was starting to revolt.

Joe agreed for us to start eating healthier and not have so much wine. He promised me he would not buy wine at the store anymore, and we would only have it when we dined out, which we would limit to the weekends.

"Great," I said. "Sounds like a perfect plan."

But Joe did not change his grocery buying habits. In fact, nothing changed. He would meet me at the door to our home with a glass of wine when he knew I had a hard day, which seemed to be most days.

"Just one glass," he would say, "to relax a bit."

But it never seemed to turn out that way as he would fill my glass when it was half empty, so I never really knew how much I was drinking. More times than not, Joe would go to the grocery store and bring back a dozen bottles of wine. Again and again, I begged him to stop. We were drinking (and eating) too much. It started to be gluttonous in my opinion. He commented that I was being ridiculous then poured me a glass of wine.

I admit, I drank more than I should have, but as time would soon tell, this was part of Joe's plan. We drank every evening, either after our exercise class or Joe would meet me at the door with a glass of wine after a hard day at the office and want to rub my shoulders. I told him we needed to stop this pattern because it was not good for our health. He would always agree, but then nothing ever changed. If I refused a glass of wine when I came home, he would get offended and have his feelings hurt. I thought to myself, *it was not worth hurting his feelings over a little glass of wine*, but ultimately, one glass turned into two or three, then a bottle or two.

CHAPTER 2

THE ENSNARING TRAP

"Keep me safe from the traps set by evildoers,
from the snares they have laid for me."
Psalm 141:9 NIV

Before I knew it, Joe had essentially moved most of his belongings in with me. He was there all the time, and we had become inseparable. I loved being with him and having his support. He placed me on a high pedestal, and I had never had this type of treatment before. He believed I could be his savior since he was mad at God for taking his wife although he insisted, he could now see some purpose in her passing. And although he missed her greatly, he realized that as sick as she was, she was finally pain free and happy.

I told Joe we could fully live life and experience things he could never dream. This was a blessing now even though he had hoped for a better outcome on that day of his wife's death more than one year ago. He agreed and seemed to be responding well to the new changes in his life. Joe had planned an amazing getaway for us so he could "officially" propose to me. What could possibly go wrong?

A DEEP, DARK SECRET

One morning before I left for work, a few weeks before we were scheduled to depart for our engagement trip, Joe seemed very distraught. When I asked him what was wrong, he confessed to me that I had hurt his feelings with something I said the previous night and that he thought we should call off the engagement. I had no idea I had misspoken, and I felt awful. I was heartbroken that he wanted to call off the engagement over this misunderstanding. I apologized over and over, but it did not seem to help. He told me that he would pack his belongings and be gone by the time I got home from work. I was distraught, but unfortunately, as much as I wished I could stay and console him further, I had to be at work for an early morning meeting I could not miss. I begged him to stay so we could talk about this further over lunch. He agreed that we could have lunch, but he was adamant on leaving after our lunch meeting.

During my meeting, I started receiving bizarre text messages from Joe in all capital letters. The messages were very dark and scary, and the last message stated I needed to come home right away. I explained that I could not leave the office until about lunch time as I was engrossed in meetings for the morning. Shortly after this last text message, I received a message with pictures of my office building and text stating that if I did not come home right away, certain people (ones I shared with Joe that had not treated me very well) would be killed one by one until I obeyed this command.

I was immediately terrified but then remembered something Joe told me several weeks back. A deep dark secret he had carried for years. He mentioned a "presence" took over his body at times. This presence was what he described as a lost soul looking to revenge wrongs done to innocent people, a vigilante of sorts. This presence was only described as the "Being" but had no specific name. Joe first encountered the "Being" when his mother was in danger when he was a young child. He explained that since that time, the "Being" showed up from time to time to wreak havoc on lawless members of society. While I did not really understand or necessarily believe what he was saying at the time, I was witnessing a manifestation of the "Being" now for the first time and was terrified.

I was unsure what to do, so I texted that I would come home right away as I was afraid this "Being" would harm people. When I arrived home, I encountered the "Being" face to face. He was wearing a suit and tie and looked a bit different from Joe's usual demeaner. I asked him where Joe was and he told me that he had put him in a safe place until his sadness could be resolved. I inquired if this sadness was caused by my words last night and the "Being" said yes. Again, I apologized over and over as that was definitely not my intent. He said that it didn't matter, and he would deal with me now. I tried to escape at this point, but he physically restrained me, which prevented me from leaving. He displayed a gun, and he said he would have no problem using it. I was not sure if he meant on me or on others, but either way, I knew I better comply.

The "Being" told me we were to go to the bank and lunch just like I had planned with Joe that day. The "Being" insisted I act normal as he wanted to see what Joe saw in me. He insisted I give no clues as to what was going on, or I would pay for it later. We ordered lunch, and I ate as much as I could under the circumstances. I noticed that the "Being" did not need glasses to see the menu as Joe always wore glasses. Also, the "Being" ate food Joe would never order. It was strange. Even though I was terrified, I was somewhat curious but knew not to push my limits with the "Being" since he did seem to show some feelings for me. He even commented that he would be the one taking me on the engagement trip. He relished traveling to vanquish any wrong doers. Once I was compliant, the "Being" seemed to be more at ease and less threatening to me personally.

After lunch, he told me I should return to work because he had things to do. I complied but was completely unsettled. Would the "Being" execute his plans of inflicting harm on others? After I returned to work, I received another text message from the "Being" telling me to delete every text he had sent, including pictures. He said he tapped my phone and would know if I forwarded them or kept them. I was so terrified I deleted all as he requested. After this, I tried to call, but there was no answer and no reply to my text for what seemed like hours.

Mid-afternoon, I received a call from Joe who stated he had some sort of accident and his finger was broken. He had sustained some cuts, but he did not remember what had happened. He thought he had passed out but then dreaded my response. I explained to him what had happened, and he was clearly despondent. Again, I made an excuse to my co-worker and told her I needed to leave a little early. I immediately went home to find Joe bleeding and bruised. His finger was broken, but he refused any treatment. He sobbed and cried over this incident for hours.

He was inconsolable as he cried out to me, "Please do not leave me, help me. I need you!"

What was I to do? I loved him and wanted to help him but could I endure this madness?

Ultimately, love won out, and I decided to try to help him. He promised this would never happen again as he could sometimes feel this presence manifesting. Joe told me that if he felt those feelings, he would immediately do things to prevent this from occurring (as if he really had any control). Joe begged me not to tell anyone about this. He was embarrassed and ashamed. He then shared many more dark secrets he experienced or the aftermath of these events, as the actual events only seemed like a shadow to him. He wanted no part of the "Being," but somehow, he could not seem to get rid of him.

This would not be my last encounter with the "Being," which I later realized was a demonic presence or multiple demons manifesting in Joe. This early act did set the precedence for what our life or should I say my life would become. The burning question (even to me) is why did I stay at this point? I cannot say for sure, but even though this did not seem right to me, I think it was my desire to help. I had fallen madly in love with him. Joe gave me a reason for living, and I prayed about him so God must have brought him into my life.

Maybe I could save him? I should at least try as it must be the right thing to do, right?

> "There's a way of life that looks harmless enough; look again—it leads straight to hell. Sure, those people appear to be having a good time, but all that laughter will end in heartbreak."
>
> PROVERBS 14:12-13

ONE EVENING IN MAUI

After that one crazy incident, everything went back to normal—even better than normal. Joe's cuts and bruises healed. His broken finger healed, and there was no talk of the "Being," as he seemed to be a million miles away now. Joe wanted us to move into a larger apartment (since he could afford it) and sell all of our belongings to start our new life together. It could be a fresh start for both of us! I could not have agreed more, so I put all the negative thoughts out of my mind. Joe asked me a while back where I thought the most romantic place on earth would be for an engagement.

I replied with little hesitation, "A romantic beach."

Joe diligently planned this extravagant trip to Maui for our engagement that also coincided with my birthday.

"Nothing but the best for my doll," he would say.

I loved it when he called me that. I was so proud to be by his side. I was shocked at the luxury of this trip. I could not get much time off from work, but he made the quick trip happen. After an amazing and funfilled flight to Maui, I had a bit of headache due to lack of food and felt a bit nauseated. Although Joe seemed a bit irritated at this, he took care of me, and within a few hours, I was back on my feet. He scheduled a private tour of the island, and although I had been to Maui a few years back with Mary, I had not had this type of experience.

The extravagance was beyond measure. Once again, I felt like Cinderella in a fairy tale. I praised God for graciously giving me such a man who put me on a pedestal, spent time with me, lavished me with meaningful gifts, and met all of my heartfelt desires. Reservations were made for the finest restaurant in Maui. I could not believe I was actually in Maui with the love of my life. How could I refuse such a romantic and amazing man? We arrived at the restaurant in our finest attire. We were early for our reservation, so we had wine before dinner. Once we were seated for our meal, no expense was spared. Again, Joe showered me with food, wine, and gifts. Despite telling him numerous times that he did not have to go to these measures to win me over, he seemed to turn a deaf ear to my pleas.

THE ENGAGEMENT

Following dinner and dessert, I excused myself to the ladies room for a few minutes. When I returned, there were a barrage of photographers and people all around our table with Joe right in the middle of the crowd, smiling from ear to ear, with flowers and a box in hand. I think half of the restaurant was watching us.

As I came closer, he got on one knee and said, "Will you marry me, my angel?"

How could I refuse?

"Of course, I will marry you my love," I replied.

The whole restaurant cheered as he placed the ring on my finger. I felt so fortunate to have a man like him. It seemed God had truly intervened on my behalf and blessed me. I felt like I was surrounded by the papparazi as the photographers snapped photo after photo. I was so overwhelmed, I broke down in tears.

Joe also teared up a bit as he said, "You have made me the happiest I have ever been in my life. Here is to forever."

He raised a glass to toast our engagement. Everything seemed too perfect at that moment and any thought of doubt disappeared from my mind.

STARTING FRESH

Once we returned home, the magic continued. Joe insisted that we begin our fresh start. He had charmed his way into the leasing office at my apartment complex and gotten us a deal on a two bedroom that was out of my budget. Joe seemed so debonair in his dealings with people. He was charming, handsome, and knew the exact words to say to people to get them to do what he wanted.

I reluctantly agreed to sell all of my furniture I had worked so hard to acquire after my divorce, but I understood his notion of starting over together. Joe was planning to sell his home and belongings as well, but his daughter from a previous marriage had been living in his home with her family, so there was no huge rush for him. He decided to help me with the process of cleaning out my old stuff to sell and make room for the new.

I appreciated the help until the day I came home and he was furious. I could not imagine what happened to make him so angry. He pulled me into the bathroom and had me look into the closet. There on the top shelf were some gifts I had stuck back from an old boyfriend.

"Why were you keeping these?" he demanded.

I explained I had forgotten they were there from more than two years prior, and I would certainly have gotten rid of them if I had remembered. He was not satisfied with that answer and accused me of still pining over the old boyfriend. I assured him that was not the case. Unfortunately, there was no reconciliation and soon enough, the "Being" returned.

I saw Joe's transformation with my own eyes. He looked in the mirror and his face contorted. His eyes changed color from brown to gray, and they became more narrow and drawn.

"How could you do this to him?" the "Being" demanded an answer.

"I forgot the items were there," I pleaded, but to no avail.

"Has he not done everything for you and treated you like a queen and yet you still keep treasures from this boyfriend?" he insisted.

I said I was sorry and that it was an oversight. I had forgotten they were there. The "Being" left my apartment, and eventually Joe returned with no memory of the encounter. He apologized and explained he was so in love with me that the thought of anyone else in my life made him go insane. Joe pleaded with me to forgive him, and I did.

This scenario played out over and over again as Joe went through all my belongings, including photos, my old computers, and phones. Joe viewed text messages from my ex-boyfriends and others. Many times following, Joe transformed into the "Being" and even went as far as to call me all kinds of names related to behaviors I never engaged in. Even though I had shared intimate secrets with Joe, he became furious that I was lying to him about my life. This was the most absurd thing I had heard. Why would I lie to the man I love and was soon to marry?

Although I loved Joe deeply, I wanted to get out at this point, but the "Being" threatened to hurt me if I even thought about leaving Joe. The "Being" seemed to like me in some weird way, even though I often enraged him. I did not know what to do at this point because I could not face this frightening thing alone. I did not even realize what or who I was dealing with when the "Being" would manifest. I was afraid to tell anyone as Joe seemed to know every move I made, and thus the "Being" knew.

A PROMISE TO CHANGE

Finally, Joe admitted to me that he was insecure, and if I would go ahead and commit to marry him this crazy behavior would stop. I agreed, and a date was set. He was not very happy that the date was several months away, but I convinced him I needed time to get things together and plan. He smiled and agreed.

After the date was set and we moved into the two bedroom apartment, things got back to normal and Joe seemed happy. The "Being" seemed to be part of his past, and he assured me everything would be different. Once we were married, he would feel secure. Again, I never spoke a word of this to anyone. If I had, would they have believed me? Joe had charmed everyone including my friends and family. They loved him and thought I was fortunate to catch him before some other woman got her hooks into him. I felt I was in too deep to undo what had been done, and Joe was so remorseful and needed my help desparately. I believed he loved me, and I knew I loved him. *Love can conquer all*, I thought, *even the demon "Being" that possessed Joe*. I had no idea what I was setting myself up for.

During this time, this pesky pain in my arms and legs continued and grew a bit worse. There were now more days when I could not even get out of bed because the pain in my legs was so bad. Additionally, it was often very difficult to lift my arms above my shoulders. For someone who was active and loved the outdoors, this seemed like a curse. Joe was very sympathetic to this condition and made sure I took my vitamins and medications. He insisted I continue to drink the protein shake and coffee he made for me every morning. He would be enraged if I did not drink the protein shake at work, so I dutifully obliged his request daily.

He insisted that he wanted me to get better so we could enjoy our life together. I struggled and no matter how much pain I was in, I got up most days and worked through the pain. This illness, whatever was causing it, was not going to interfere with my life. How could I turn my back and become a burden on this man who was giving me everything I had always wanted? He was a gift from God.

JOSHUA

Several months before the wedding, I wanted Joe to meet my youngest son, Joshua. Joshua and his wife were living in St. Louis at the time. They had only been married a few years and had no children. Joshua struggled with depression, and we soon learned he and his wife were separated. He was also really struggling with his job, so I thought it would be a good time to visit and see if we could offer any help.

Joe immediately felt sympathetic toward Joshua and took him under his wing. When Joshua's marriage seemed that it would finally break up, Joe invited him to come back home and stay with us until he could get back on his feet. Once Joshua tied up a few loose ends, he took Joe up on his offer. I was thrilled to have Joshua back home. I was so impressed with Joe's concern and care of Joshua during this critical time and repeatedly thanked him for his support. Joe would say, it was the least he could do as he always wanted a son. Now he had the best of both worlds. He would soon have a wonderful wife and then her son would be like a son to him. Joshua's father had not always been there for him and I knew Joe would be a great influence on Joshua.

During our visit to see Joshua, the pain in my arms increased significantly. I felt helpless not knowing what to do. Joe insisted that perhaps when we return home, I should go see a doctor. I reluctantly agreed, as I did not like this feeling that I was unable to move without significant pain. Although the pain seemed somewhat intermittent, it was starting to become an everyday occurrence. Joe was always there. I was so thankful for him.

THE LONG-AWAITED HOMECOMING

Finally, about two months after our visit, Joshua came to live with us. Although he was still separated from his wife, she also came to the area and got a job. She lived about an hour away and continued to care deeply for Joshua. I could tell Joshua's depression was growing worse, and part of this was the fact that he had left his job back in St. Louis and now was just sitting at home with nothing really to do except focus on his problems. I encouraged him to find a job, but then he reminded me he didn't have a car. Joshua and his wife shared a car, and she took it in the separation as she was the one who needed to go back and forth to work now. Joshua was left with a motorcycle, but in the sprawling metropolitan area in which we lived, it was not a good option for commuting.

Joe quickly volunteered to take Joshua around, including to work if needed. Joshua was a little hesitant to take Joe up on his offer, as he did not want to be a burden, but ultimately decided this might be a good temporary option for his situation. Joshua went to work, albeit not an ideal job, but at least he was doing something.

Joshua and Joe started to bond somewhat, but then their personalities started to clash. I told Joshua he needed to be thankful to Joe for taking him to work, regardless of any personality clashes. He should be appreciative and respectful to him. Joe started to complain to me about Joshua at the same time. Joe insisted that Joshua was throwing his life away and that he was rude and ungrateful to him. It seemed that my vision of a happy family was slowly fading away, but I did my best to keep the peace between the two. I continued to tell Joe that he should be an example to Joshua as he was still in the aftermath of depression. Joe would always agree and promise to do better, but then it seemed things would go right back to where they had been before.

Throughout this time, I do not think Joshua and Joe ever exchanged words. They just both complained to me about the other one. Over time, Joshua seemed to feel a bit better, and his depression was waning. He started going out with some friends and would often hang out with his wife. Sometimes, Joshua's wife would visit for the weekend, which I felt was positive since he had been so isolated prior to this. Although I was not sure they could ever reconcile, I prayed for them both. I had always liked Joshua's wife and thought she was a good influence on him but knew there were other issues I did not see.

ALL IS NOT WHAT IT SEEMS

As our wedding drew closer, Joe seemed a bit agitated. I often asked him what was wrong, and he would reply that he was tired of waiting for me to be his wife. I assured him we were going to get married and everything would be fine. Besides, I still had lots of preparation to make. It is not every day a girl marries Prince Charming, after all. While he seemed to be reassured with these comments, his anxiety would return from time to time.

Joe and I bought new furniture for our two-bedroom apartment after I had sold all my belongings. We had picked out the furniture and décor together. It was perfect and quite expensive, but Joe insisted that no price was too high as long as his little doll was happy. Despite Joe's brief period of cooking at home, we started to go out to eat almost every night again, even after I had begged for us to eat healthier due to my painful condition. But he had his favorite places and insisted we go to support his newfound friends.

Joe got to know all the managers of our favorite restaurants and was treated like royalty when he arrived. He always got the best tables, and I was impressed at the way he finessed the staff and managers. As we continued to wine and dine excessively, my weight continued to balloon up. I did my best to remain active despite my ailments, but Joe continued to insist that he liked me better this way. While I was not happy with the added weight, I felt helpless to change our habits. Joe insisted that we keep going out because he enjoyed the social aspect as well as the royal treatment from those who catered to him.

I started noticing that Joe's newly made friends seemed to only be around when he was spending money. When I asked if I could meet some of his old friends, those he had before he met me, he told me they abandoned him when his wife died, and it was very painful as he had to spend all that time alone. I was extremely sympathetic to this situation, as I experienced some of the same when I divorced my first husband. I told him I was sure they just felt uncomfortable and did not know what to say to him. He did think this was true, but it was still quite painful to him.

He always added, "Now I have your friends."

I agreed—my friends did adore him.

BREAKING FAMILY TIES

Joe knew how much I desired to be close to my children. Joe would often berate them by posting insulting comments on their social media posts. I asked him politely to not do this, to which he replied, they should not be so stupid. I agreed some things should not have been posted but that he should ignore these just as I did. He insisted their posts made me look bad, and he was just defending my honor. One of these events escalated with my daughter. She called during one of our wine drinking weekends and demanded an explanation. I told her the comment was Joe's opinion, and I had nothing to do with it. I defended

Joe's right to his opinions just as much as she had a right to post hers. This particular incident blew over, but there would soon be many more.

As Joe continued to nag me about my children, the situation intensified. If I were to mention anything about his daughter (who paid no rent, did not work, and lived in his home with her family), he would get very angry. There was no winning this argument. Ultimately he tried to convince me he was all I had. I should cling to him alone because my children were unreliable. At the time, my elderly parents lived far away, so he took every opportunity to point out that they never called me, and they cared for my brothers and sisters more than me. If I could not see all of this, then I was clearly not all there. I must be living in a fantasy world, as Joe would say.

Maybe Joe was right? We only had each other. My children had their own lives now and did not have time for me. Additionally, my brothers and sisters all seemed to be in a better place than me, and I could see what Joe was saying about how my parents treated me. I had always been the black sheep of the family and now it was becoming more and more obvious to me.

But is this enough to cut all ties? According to Joe, I should only cling to him. While I considered my options, I could never give up on my children. Even though Joe's comments seemed valid, they were not enough to convince me.

Joe seemed to be close to his daughter but in a way that was more controlling of her than affectionate. He confided in me that her mother remarried shortly after their divorce and that his daughter grew reserved and shy, so he wanted to help her stand up for herself. He regretted that he was somewhat of an absent father, as he had to work two jobs to pay child support, and then pay his second wife's medical bills. Once he advanced to an executive level, he was able to step into his daughter's life but she was a teen by this time.

She married right after high school and did not go to college. Joe felt responsible for this decision. While he seemed to like her husband, he often commented to me that he thought he was lazy and useless and that his daughter would be better off without him. I always thought his comment was unfounded, as Joe's son-in-law worked and his daughter stayed home (mostly in bed). But I kept my opinion to myself. During our time together, I never really got to know her well or her family. Joe tended to keep me isolated from her, and only once was I allowed to help her, which I share about later.

SETTING THE TRAP

"You're from your father, the Devil, and all you want to do is please him. He was a killer from the very start. He couldn't stand the truth because there wasn't a shred of truth in him. When the Liar speaks, he makes it up out of his lying nature and fills the world with lies."

JOHN 8:44

In hindsight, I realize Joe was laying the foundation for what was to come in the not so distant future. He was setting the trap by isolating me from my family, making me completely dependent on him, keeping me on booze, and controlling my every thought and move. He now controlled almost everything in my life, but I was blinded by love.

We had truly become inseparable. The only place I ever went alone was to work, and he would often drive me there. At first, I was thrilled to have someone who showed so much interest in everything I did and put me on a pedestal. If I met friends for a girls' lunch, he would either insist on attending or drive me there and pick me up. He took endless photos of me and posted them on social media because he wanted everyone to be jealous of his beautiful bride-to-be. He wanted all of his old friends who scoffed at him when his wife had died to see he moved on and was living a dream life. If I ever went anywhere alone, Joe constantly texted me to make sure I was doing alright. I used to laugh and tell him,"How did I ever manage my life before you came along?"

As far as our finances went, I paid all the bills, and Joe gave me the money for half of the rent at first, but he did pay for all groceries, going out to eat, trips, and other related items. He would often go shopping while I was at work, so I never knew what type of new gadget or article of clothing I would come home to find. For example, one day, he showed up with two teacup puppies that were littermates. He knew I had always wanted to get a small dog but hadn't because of work and travel. Joe insisted that the two dogs would keep each other company. He decided these two were my dogs, and within a week, he purchased himself a small dog as well. I questioned him numerous times about his spending habits. It did seem that he had an endless supply of money and that we were never in need of anything.

 He would always tell me, "Relax, I have plenty of money."

I can see now that Joe wanted the life I lived with my friends and family. Joe was very charasmatic and people were naturally drawn to him, including my friends. I could not imagine why his previous friends treated him so bad following his wife's death. I assumed this was probably not quite the accurate portrayal of the situation. I also wondered if Joe was the one who did not continue the relationships because they were friends of both his deceased wife's and him.

Joe completely mesmorized my friends from my exercise classes, especially the dance classes. He became "one of the girls," and they would include him in all the gossip and parties they had. The girls would often comment that they wished their husbands were like Joe. Joe loved the attention. It was a match made in heaven. He had integrated himself into every inch of my life. At the time, I could not have been happier.

TRIPS TO NOWHERE

About once a week, Joe would disappear all day long. I had no idea where he went. Joshua would tell me Joe would leave right after I went to work and then show back up just in time to take him to work in the late afternoon. While I was a little relieved to have a few moments to myself, albeit, at work, I became concerned over his whereabouts. When I asked Joe about this, he would tell me he did not remember being gone, and perhaps the "Being" had taken over his body, as he would return covered in dirt at times. I became more and more concerned about these episodes, but Joe assured me all was well, and he thought the "Being" was removing items from Joe's home in preparation for his departure—his "permanent" departure from Joe's life.

Joe continued to move things into our new apartment on a weekly basis, so I assumed most of his disappearances were related to cleaning out his home and preparing for our life together. One day when I returned home from work, I noticed Joe had brought in numerous weapons from his home. The weapons included all types of guns, swords, and knives. Among the guns were automatic rifles, numerous handguns, and silencers. When I inquired about all these weapons, he told me it was better not to ask as they belonged to the "Being."

I was terrified and asked would it be possible to store these in our storage unit instead of the apartment? Joe agreed and placed all of these weapons in storage, except for his swords and a handgun he kept under the bed for protection. Joe assured me he felt more secure and comfortable if he had someway to defend himself against an unwanted attacker.

As I look back on these episodes now, I wonder to myself, how could I have been so naïve to not see his plan? But there was more to come, much more.

I WILL BE YOUR CAREGIVER

As time went on, I became more and more disillusioned with this ongoing terrible pain in my extremities. I was still active and attended my exercise classes, but my mobility was severely limited. I would often cry due to the excruciating pain and the lack of ability to move my arms or legs. I decided to visit my primary care doctor to voice my complaints. As always, Joe was right by my side as the visit was more of a social call to him.

My doctor ordered bloodwork and determined I had been struck down by an autoimmune disease as there were markers for this in my blood. Joe seemed quite surprised but encouraged me to follow up on this. My doctor gave me massive doses of steroids to try to reduce the pain in my extremities and to give me back some range of motion. While this helped, the medication came with terrible side effects. My face was almost contorted as it was hugely swollen, and my whole body looked puffy. With the wedding a few weeks away now, I was not sure what to do.

I discovered a large knot near the front part of my shoulder. I panicked and immediately called my doctor who referred me right away to have it examined further. Upon examination and aspiration, the knot was benign. It was only a fluid filled cavity with no known cause.

"These things happen from time to time," my doctor explained to Joe and me, "you are fine, so do not worry."

I was relieved but now had a huge bruise extending down the front of my shoulder onto my chest. It was quite obvious in my wedding dress, so I was very discouraged and disappointed. I questioned whether to postpone the wedding due to my health, but Joe became infuriated when I suggested this. After all, he had waited more than nine months to marry me and refused to wait another minute longer. I saw his reaction as comforting. He wanted to marry me no matter what the circumstances. Joe wanted to care for me, even if I ended up being sick and unable to care for myself after the wedding.

He explained, "I have an abundance of experience caring for a sick spouse, but I know this will not happen to you."

How prophetic his words would turn out to be.

"Work hard for sin your whole life and your pension is death. But God's gift is real life, eternal life, delivered by Jesus, our Master."

ROMANS 6:23

CHAPTER 3

THE DEADLY PLOT

"The heart is hopelessly dark and deceitful, a puzzle that no one can figure out. But I, God, search the heart and examine the mind. I get to the heart of the human. I get to the root of things. I treat them as they really are, not as they pretend to be."
Jeremiah 17:9-10

READY OR KNOT

With the trap set, the next event on Joe's agenda was to put his ultimate plan into action. Although Maui had been the perfect sight for the proposal, due to lack of availability, the wedding was set at the next best thing—a beach setting in the Florida Keys. Joe loved the beach, and I did too. It was to be the perfect setting for a perfect day.

As the wedding day loomed near, the anxiety of the day seemed to engulf us both. While I continued to suffer from medical problems, Joe was busy with preparations for the day, making sure everything was perfect. We were thrilled to learn a few weeks before the wedding that my best friend, Mary, and her husband, Dan, could attend the wedding. They were such a huge part of my life, and I was thrilled they could be there to celebrate with us. What a blessing! They had come to care deeply for Joe as well.

We boarded our flight to Florida and off we went. I could not believe my eyes when I saw the resort Joe selected. It was a beautiful setting, and the staff was overwhelmingly accommodating to him. Immediately, upon our arrival, Joe insisted on champagne for everyone, even though it was before lunch. How could I refuse? It was a time of celebration, and I felt just like Cinderella. We were set to be married the next morning and then have a few days to celebrate before we went back home. Due to the time of year, we had to wait a bit for the honeymoon but that did not seem to matter much. The best thing is that I would be married to the man of my dreams.

The morning of our wedding finally came, and I was so nervous. Joe went out with Dan that morning, and we agreed to meet up again at the aisle. We had both written our own vows, so I could not wait to see what he would say. I busied myself with Mary's help in getting dressed, as I wanted to look beautiful for Joe. Joe had a bottle of champagne and orange juice as well as all types of breakfast croissants delivered to the room. He left implicit instructions with Mary to make sure I drank the protein shake he left and then to indulge in the breakfast.

I was so nervous I could barely eat. Mary encouraged me to at least drink some of the protein shake for a bit of energy because we had a long day ahead. I drank a little bit of the protein shake and then had a bit of Champagne to relax my nerves. I could not figure out why I was so nervous. I was marrying the man of my dreams.

The wedding was beautiful and went off without a hitch. It was settled; Joe and I were now husband and wife. I could not believe how amazing I felt. I had never seen Joe so happy. He wrote such heartfelt and romantic vows, which he memorized. I felt a little intimidated as my vows were not near as romantic as his, and I was so nervous I had to read mine. Joe did not seem to care. He was floating on cloud nine. What could possibly go wrong with this enchanted day?

Joe arranged a special lunch for the four of us after the ceremony. We headed to the venue, but Joe insisted on stopping for drinks before we had lunch to celebrate. We ended up having several drinks before lunch, but everything was so perfect I did not complain. When we arrived at the lunch venue, we had more drinks before lunch. By this time, I was feeling a bit woozy, but Joe insisted it was only because I had not eaten. I ordered lunch but only ate a small amount because I did not want to feel sick on this special day. He ordered more drinks, and although I knew better, I partook as I did not want to upset him. My friends commented how blessed I was to now have a wonderful husband like Joe, who treated me so well after my previous husband had been so abusive. I agreed wholeheartedly and gave Joe a kiss.

Late in the afternoon, I told Joe I really needed a nap before dinner as I felt extremely sick from all the drinks and the little bit of food. We went back to our hotel room and made plans to meet our friends later that evening for dinner. When we got back to the hotel room, I immediately became ill. Joe took this opportunity to criticize me for my behavior.

"How could you behave this way and talk about your ex-husband on our wedding day?" he raged.

I tried to explain that I was lifting him up based on my friends' compliments to him. Joe heard none of this and told me to go to bed. He murmured what a huge mistake he had made in marrying me and that he knew better. I was nothing but a washed up old drunk and he was the best I would ever have. He told me I was already so old that the only thing I could hope for now was death. I laid in the bed and cried, too sick to get up and walk out. Plus, where would I go?

I was shocked at Joe's behavior. Clearly this marked a turning point in our relationship. I thought once we were married, all of this would stop. What a lie.

THE WEDDING NIGHT

As Joe lay beside me, I apologized to him over and over. I explained I should have eaten more and drank less. I let him know how sorry I was that I hurt his feelings by my response to the comments about my ex-husband. Finally, he told me to just go to sleep and forget about it.

"Some wedding night," Joe commented as he went to sleep.

It was all my fault, and I promised him I would make it up to him. He grunted with no real response. I drifted off to sleep as the illness and drowsiness from the alcohol overtook me.

When I awoke, Joe was getting dressed. He commented for me to call my friends and tell them we were not going to make dinner. I asked him where he was going, and he replied, "Out!"

I knew better than to respond when he was in this mood and had this attitude. I certainly did not want to stir up the "Being" here. I started to cry inconsolably and begged him not to go. He replied that I needed to hush up and call my friends. I dried my tears long enough to make the call as Joe stormed out. I let Mary know I was feeling too sick to make dinner, and she laughed and told me that she and Dan had already made other plans because they figured this was the case. Mary asked if everything was okay, and I told her I had upset Joe and then apologized to her for messing up the plans. Mary laughed and said not to worry about it. It was my wedding day, and Joe would get over it. I laughed a bit, but somehow, I knew Joe would *never* get over it.

Joe returned to our hotel room in the wee hours of the morning. I did not ask where he had gone. I only apologized again and again. He replied that I should go to sleep, and we could talk in the morning. I asked if he was ok, and he said he was better now. I was not quite sure what that meant but I had an idea. He certainly deserved better than me. How could this have happened? How could I have been so careless with my drinking? I finally married the man of my dreams, and I blew it. What could I do to fix this?

The morning came and I awoke feeling much better. Joe was still asleep, and I leaned over and kissed him gently. He slowly awoke and hugged me.

"How did you sleep, doll?" he asked.

"I slept ok," I said.

I again apologized to him, and he said, "Well, I suppose you should make it up to me, huh?"

He grabbed and started to tickle me. We kissed deeply, as he rolled me over onto him. It seemed all had been forgiven. We got out of bed, and I phoned my friends. We agreed to meet for breakfast before they took a flight back home. Joe and I had a few days to spend in the Keys, and we planned to enjoy it, but I knew things were now different with him. He had forgiven me for the wedding night, but something was still amiss. I just could not quite put my finger on it.

THE RECEPTION

When we returned home from the wedding, everything seemed to go back to normal, or I should say the normalcy of Joe's unstable moods. We planned a reception for a month later with our friends and family and were looking forward to it. Joe's daughter even promised to attend with her family. I was excited as I was never quite sure if she ever left her home. She seemed like a very dark and troubled soul.

My children were excited to meet her. Rachel commented that she had always wanted to have a sister instead of two dusty old brothers. Joe seemed to embrace his belonging, and I was so happy we were now a family. It seemed like everything would work out despite the awful wedding night.

We held the reception in our home. We had catered food, cake, and wine of all sorts. It was an elaborate celebration. Joe pulled all the strings with his restaurant contacts, so we had the best of everything. Joshua played emcee that night and introduced us to the crowd as we entered the party. It was spectacular. At one point, I noticed Joe's daughter had not yet arrived. I mentioned this to Joe, and he called her.

She apparently got lost and decided to return home. I could see the disappointment on Joe's face, but he quickly recovered and moved on to visit with our guests. I also noticed none of Joe's friends were in attendance as I had looked forward to meeting them. I asked if he had heard anything from them, and he told me that he was not surprised they did not attend. He said they were just jealous of him. I thought at the time it was an unusual comment, but I decided it was Joe's way of dealing with the disappointment, so I dropped the subject.

"Besides," Joe commented as he pointed to the crowd of my friends, "*my friends are here.*"

THE TRIP OF A LIFETIME

Shortly after the reception, Joe received an invitation to go on an exclusive trip throughout Europe due to his elaborate spending on jewelry and art during our mountain vacation. I was impressed by this offer, and Joe decided we would go. I would have to miss three weeks of work, but this was the trip of a lifetime. I was so excited and managed to get time off from work for those three weeks, so we began to plan for the trip. I could not believe the connections Joe had with this group, as we had all our accommodations paid including airfare. I was a little concerned as I asked Joe what this group wanted in return. Were we required to purchase certain items or spend a certain amount of money? He told me to relax; he had it covered.

When we arrived at the initial destination, Joe was his debonair and charming self as always. He did warn me not to embarrass him with my drunkenness and inappropriate behavior. I was not sure why he told me this in such a harsh manner, because all I could recall was the wedding night.

The first night of the trip, Joe treated me horribly. It was the wedding night all over again, although this time, I kept the drinking in check. He told me he regretted marrying me as I was nothing compared to his former wife.

I asked him, "If you truly feel this way, why are we here?"

He looked at me and said, "I do not really know."

In what seemed like a moment of clarity for him, Joe went on to say, "I guess you are right when you say that I could not love someone and talk to them as I do you. You will never be my wife. My wife is dead."

I was so hurt by his comments that I cried the entire night and wanted to return home, but I had three more weeks of this vacation to endure. How would I survive?

With the truth finally out, the remainder of the trip seemed to go as best as could be expected. Joe put on an air of nobility, but I saw right through him. He treated me well during this time, but I had a bad feeling. We saw many sites throughout Europe, and I learned a great deal about music, jewelry, and art. Joe purchased items during the trip, and I became concerned as to the cost of these.

On the last day, we had to settle our bill with the host company. Joe informed me that I was to put a deposit of about ten thousand dollars on my credit card for his purchases, but he would transfer money to me to cover it. I agreed, as there was no other choice, according to Joe. He told me his funds were tied up but would have them available in a matter of weeks when we returned home. I had never asked about his finances because he always seemed to have money to spend. I started to have doubts about his never-ending finances but kept my mouth shut and did as I was told.

ESCALATED ANGER

When we returned from the trip, Joe's anger seemed to get more and more out of control. He would tell me that nothing about me was real and I was a hypocrite because I pretended like I wanted to be healthy but was nothing more than a drunk piece of trash. Joe said I was a consolation prize for him as his true wife had died, so now, he was stuck with me. He lamented over her day and night, and while I tried to help him by being there for him and telling him I loved him, he just became angrier and angrier. He would yell at me, saying that I was fat, ugly, old, and undesirable. What happened to my perfect life with Prince Charming? I was devastated at the turn our life was taking.

Then came the threats. If I did not immediately respond to his text messages or phone calls while I was working, he would go into a rage. The more I tried to assure him and love him, the worse things got. He would say the only thing that would make him happy was to find me dead. He also threatened that if I ever told anyone or acted like there was any problem outside of our home, he would go after Joshua and kill him in his sleep.

Then the violence started. At first, it was shoves or pushes, but soon he would twist my arms around so hard I thought they would break. He would hold me down and put a pillow over my face, then remove it and laugh. He would tell me that he held my life and death in his hands. Even though Joshua was two rooms away, Joe would drag me into the bedroom to slap, choke, and punch me at his will. If I made a sound, he threatened to assassinate Joshua. Then, he told me he would go after my other children.

He described in detail how he would keep me barely alive, just long enough so I could see the heads of my grandchildren displayed at my feet for all my sins. I was terrified but had no choice except to do as he asked. No one knew of the violence and abuse I was enduring on a now daily basis under Joe's rage. From the outside, all seemed normal; we were a happily married newlywed couple.

YOU SHOULD BE ASHAMED

One Friday night, we met Mary and Dan for dinner. We had a wonderful time, and Joe seemed to be in good spirits or so I thought. That night when we arrived home, we greeted Joshua and his wife, who was visiting, and made plans to go to breakfast with them the following morning. Joe suddenly announced that we were tired and going to bed. I said my goodnights to Joshua and his wife and retired to the bedroom, knowing all too well what Joe meant.

I do not even remember what had made him so angry at this point, but by this time in the relationship, the fact that I was still breathing made Joe mad. He unleashed such rage on me by slapping and punching me repeatedly in the face. He would tell me to move my hand when I would try to protect myself from the onslaught of the beating. If I did not move my hand, he threatened he would go in right now with his gun and execute Joshua and his wife. I moved my hand and took the beating. Finally, Joe must have gotten tired or saw that this beating would be difficult to cover up if he continued, so he stopped.

He climbed into bed with his gun and stuck it under my chin and said, "Give me a reason to kill you, please!"

I did not move or make a sound all night. This was the worst beating I had endured so far. The next morning when we awoke, Joe commanded that I get up and let him look at my face. My eye was bruised and almost swollen shut. He told me to go put makeup on to cover up the bruising, as I should be ashamed. I was ashamed. I did not know what I had done to cause such rage, but at this point, I could feel my spirit breaking. I was beginning to have no more will to live. If I die, I reasoned, Joe will take everything, as he made me change my will and beneficiaries all to him, but at least my children would be safe, and I would no longer be in this miserable life of agony.

YIELDING TO THE DEMANDS OF A MADMAN

By this time, Joe's rage and rants continued almost daily. He was angry all the time at me for any reason. He would even make up reasons to be mad at me. One day when I came home from work, he announced to me that he was broke and demanded I withdraw my 401K and obtain money from my credit cards to give to him. He needed to be able to provide for his daughter. When I balked at the plan, he criticized me and said I was his wife, and I should help him as he had spent his fortune on me already. I told him that legally I could not touch my 401K, but I could withdraw money on my credit cards and give to him.

Joe seemed to be satisfied with that answer and told me he would pay me back as soon as he sold his house. I was shocked since Joe had postponed the selling of his home for some months now. His daughter and her family lived there, and it was where he had lived with his deceased wife. It held such great memories for him. I asked him if he was sure about selling the house, and he commented that he had no choice at this point.

I did as Joe requested and went to the bank where I had a credit card and withdrew about five thousand dollars and gave it to him. I was now afraid that I would go into bankruptcy because I was not sure how I could pay all this back on top of the other expenses Joe had me pay.

I told Joe I would help with the move, so he asked me to make the arrangements for a rental home for his daughter and her family to live in once the house was sold. Most of Joe's time was now spent cleaning things out of his home. The realtor told him he could leave nothing in the home once it sold. I think this angered Joe as he could not understand why anyone would not want the items he so highly valued.

I would never know what to expect from Joe when I arrived home. Some days, he seemed okay other days, he was in a rage and told me it was my fault he had to sell his home. As the days drew near for the house to go on the market, Joe grew angrier and angrier at me. The beatings continued almost nightly, and the next day, I would put makeup over the bruises and go to work. I was careful to avoid as many people as possible so they would not see any signs of abuse. Joe was clearly getting more violent, and I felt helpless. I knew if I left him, it would mean certain death. He had promised to torture and kill me, then move on to Joshua. I could not let this happen.

TURNING A BLIND EYE

Joe's realtor got his house ready, and within weeks, it was on the market. Joe made a point of being there any time someone looked at the house. Finally, the realtor told him this was not a good idea and begin to schedule visits at the last minute, so Joe could not make it. Even though his daughter was there at the house, she never offered any help or assistance during this time. Finally, after about a month on the market, Joe got word that the house was under contract and the closing would be within the next four weeks. The realtor again informed Joe he had to remove all items from the house by the time of the closing, so he better get busy.

Joe was unsure what to do with the larger items, so I told him that perhaps it might be best to call an estate sale expert to see if they could sell the items for him. He seemed to like that idea and within days, had an appointment with an agency that managed estate sells. Meanwhile, I found a rental home for his daughter and hired a moving company to move her family's belongings. Since Joe did not have a job, I had to sign on the lease for this house. I was hesitant, which made Joe angry, but he assured me he would pay all her expenses. I felt as if I had no choice in the matter, so I just did it.

Joe continued to work in the house several days a week, and as the deadline approached, he scheduled the estate sale. Joe agreed that whatever was not sold, he would either donate to charity or move into a storage unit. On the weekend before the closing, Joshua and I agreed to go to Joe's home to help him get the final items packed into a moving van. I would also be there to help his daughter with the moving company. Everything seemed to be coming together for the realtor's timeline.

The day before the scheduled move, I had an eye doctor appointment. It was an annual checkup, so I assumed it would be routine. Of course, Joe was with me, as he would not allow me to go anywhere alone except to work. I noticed the doctor was going in and out of the room more frequently than normal. I shrugged my shoulders and looked at Joe as if to say, "I wonder what is going on?" He looked puzzled also. Finally, the doctor came back to the room and sat down.

He said, "I have some concerning news for you."

The doctor went on to explain that I had what appeared to be a detached retina. He told us that this condition was very serious as I could lose my vision.

"I have scheduled you for an emergency appointment tomorrow morning with a retina specialist," he continued, "please do not eat or drink anything after midnight as you may be required to have emergency surgery to fix the problem."

I was in shock.

Joe immediately piped up and said, "That is not going to work for us as I am moving tomorrow."

The doctor explained that waiting was not an option, as I must go to the appointment tomorrow because I could lose my vision any moment.

I was terrified, and Joe was angry. We left the doctor's office, and Joe yelled at me, "Just great, you ruin everything!"

When we arrived home, we told Joshua of the news. Joe was angry and yelling about the situation.

"You are going to have to postpone that doctor visit tomorrow," snapped Joe, "the closing on the house cannot be postponed."

Joshua intervened and said, "I have a plan, Joe. I can take Mom to the eye doctor in the morning, and you can head to your home. As soon as Mom finishes her appointment and we know what they are going to do, I can come and help you. Then, when we finish, if Mom is having surgery, we can go up to the hospital and be with her."

Joe seemed to be okay with that plan. He commented, "As long as I get to remove my belongings, get my daughter moved, and close on my house, I am okay with the plan. I will need to take your credit card, Hope."

The next day, Joshua took me to the doctor appointment. "Joe is just nervous about selling his house," I explained to Joshua. "I am sorry about this," I told Joshua.

"No problem, Mom," he said, "I was planning on helping Joe anyway, as he had asked me some time ago."

I waited at the doctor's office for what seemed like an eternity but finally a nurse called my name. As I went back, Joshua told me that he would wait for me. I was terrified as to what this doctor would say. What if I needed surgery? Joe would be so angry. I did not want to go blind, but would it be worth the risk of being beaten or killed? It seemed like there was not a satisfactory answer to any of these questions.

The nurse asked me if I had any recent traumatic injuries to my eye. My mind went immediately to the numerous beatings that Joe had inflicted.

"No," I lied.

I could not disclose I was married to a monster. What would she think? The nurse checked my vision and put dilation drops in them and took me to a dark room to wait for the doctor. After the seemingly endless wait that was probably only thirty minutes, the doctor came in. He examined my eyes and then told me there was a small area where my retina was starting to detach. He said we could watch it for a while and see if it would heal on its own or continue to detach. The doctor gave me all the warning signs to look for if the situation became dire and said we were lucky we caught this early, so I could hopefully avoid surgery. I immediately felt relief, but then I worried as to what Joe would think or say. I knew if the assaults continued, I would go blind from the retina becoming fully detached.

Joshua and I drove to Joe's home to help him with packing up the remainder of his items. Joe did not ask what had happened or how I was. He only barked that it was about time we got there to help, as I was needed to pay for his daughter's moving expenses. Joshua intervened and explained to Joe that there was no reason to be angry or upset.

"Mom and I had a long wait, and thank God she did not have to have surgery," commented Joshua, "but now we are here to help, so we will finish up with everything that was needed so you could make the closing on your home."

I went in the house to find his daughter to see if she had everything packed to move. She was asleep, as usual, even though it was almost noon and had not packed a thing. I explained to her that the movers were going to be here soon, so she needed to start boxing up things to move. She got up and started packing up her family's belongings. I went outside and told Joe that she had not packed anything yet, and I woke her up. He burned with anger at his daughter.

"She is working on it now," I explained, "so we will make it. Do not worry."

About that time, the movers pulled up. I instructed them to follow me and took them to the areas where they could start loading the furniture. I then went up and told Joe's daughter they had arrived, so as soon as she got items boxed up to let the movers know.

Despite the morning of the doctor's visit for the partially detached retina, we finished moving Joe's daughter and cleaned out Joe's house by nightfall. We were all exhausted and headed home. I followed Joe and Joshua in the moving van to the storage unit where they dropped off a final load of Joe's belongings. We returned the van and went home. The evening was uneventful, and Joe seemed to be happy that things worked out. Joe asked me if I drank my protein shake that he made me after I left the doctor's office.

"Yes, sweetie, I did," I said.

"Good," smiled Joe, "you know I do care about what happens to you."

The next morning, I awoke, and I could not move to get out of bed as my legs hurt so bad.

"Do you think it was because of the move?" Joe asked.

"No," I answered, "I don't think so as I did not really move anything."

"Do not worry," said Joe, "I will take care of you. It is probably your illness that is coming back again."

Later that morning, I did manage to get up and move around for a few minutes, but the pain was excruciating. *Maybe I should return to the doctor again*, I thought to myself. I hated the feeling of being helpless like this. I knew Joe would not tolerate this type of situation very long, so I had to get back on my feet.

SHAKE, SHAKE, SHAKE

One morning, about two weeks after Joe's move, I was in my office sipping the coffee Joe had made me, and I noticed a greenish residue on the lid. *That is weird*, I thought to myself, but then when I examined the inside of the lid, the whole inside was green. I took a picture and texted it to Joe. He said the green residue and coloring were from the pods he used in the dishwasher, and it was fine. I thanked him and told him I just wanted to check with him. I thanked him for making me the coffee and protein shake every day, as I knew how much he really loved me.

"Of course," he replied, "anything for my doll."

I became immediately suspicious of his intentions. Over the next few weeks, I stopped drinking the protein shakes and coffee he prepared. Instead, I poured them out at work. The ongoing pain in my arms and legs started to get a little bit better, and I was able to move without as much pain. I noticed that it got increasingly better each week that I did not drink the protein shake and coffee.

One day, I arrived home from work and Joe was there, angry as ever.

"Why have you been lying to me about drinking your protein shakes?" he demanded.

"What are you talking about?" I asked curiously.

He told me he knew I had poured the shakes out when I got to work. I told him over and over that was not true. He told me I would now be required to drink the shakes every morning before I left the house, as he could no longer trust me to drink them while I was at work.

"Honey," I said, "You know I am always running late."

This seemed to momentarily satisfy him, and he continued to make the shakes for me to take to work. He told me that if he ever found out I was not drinking them, he would leave me.

"Do not be ridiculous," I said, "leave me over that?"

But he was serious as he commented, "If you do not care about your wellbeing then neither do I, and I do not want to be married to someone like that."

Surprisingly, he did not push the issue, but the violence and threats, which had been a bit calmer over the last few weeks, once again escalated very quickly. I knew in my heart that Joe was trying to poison me. But why?

NOWHERE TO ESCAPE

Night after night, I suffered horrible abuse, including slaps, punches to the face, and threats of death. I slept with a loaded gun under my chin every night and was told that if I tried to escape, Joe would go into Joshua's bedroom and kill him. Joe would often tell me he was going to push me off the third-story balcony and tell everyone I committed suicide. There were a number of times he actually held me over the third-floor balcony and threatened to drop me. He described how he would force me to write a suicide note, and then, as all my family gathered in support of his loss, he would take every dime of my retirement money.

He would have plenty of money then, and no one would know any different.

"What a sad situation—widowed twice," he would laugh.

I was terrified and lived in constant fear. And just when I thought the situation was bad, it got worse. One night, as the nightmare that was my life continued to unfold, Joe transformed into the "Being," or at this point, it might have been Joe. It was hard to tell the difference anymore. He grabbed my Bible from the nightstand and threw it down.

"You will not be needing this anymore," he yelled. "I cannot stand that thing in my presence another moment. You will denounce God and bow to me or die."

I was terrified. I prayed silently that God would help me.

"I will never denounce God," I replied, "nor bow to you."

Lord, help me!

"You will pay for this," Joe said, as he slapped my face hard.

I remained silent, but I would not bow to him or renounce God. I knew this was the end. Joe would certainly kill me. Thank God Joshua was not at home. Miraculously, as I prayed, Joe seemed to calm down. Although I received more punches and he threw my Bible in the dumpster, I somehow survived that incident. I prayed that the Lord would change Joe's heart but mostly that God would protect me and my family from this monster. I did not realize until much later that I had dealt with the devil face to face that night. God heard my cries and prevailed.

HIS FAMILY CONNECTION

I tried everything to make Joe happy so that maybe he would not harm Joshua or me. I suggested we take a trip to visit his sister. He talked to her on the phone quite often and expressed his feelings about how he missed her since she got married and moved away. His sister and I secretly planned a trip for us to visit. The plan was that we would tell Joe on the next call so we could both see his surprise. We planned activities during our visit, and I rented a car so I could drive everyone around so Joe would have time to visit with his sister. His sister, her husband, and I all took time off work to make this happen.

During the next phone call, we sprung the surprise on Joe. He seemed overjoyed when he was talking with her. They made all kinds of plans, and Joe seemed thrilled to be able to see her again. Once we hung up the phone from his sister, I could not help but smile as Joe had seemed so happy. He turned to me in a fit of rage and slapped me hard across my face.

"How dare you?" he yelled.

As I grabbed my throbbing cheek, I started to cry.

"I thought you would be happy. I am sorry. We can cancel the trip. I will say I got sick again."

"It's too late for that," Joe murmured. "You two have all the plans made."

"Joe," I begged, "I just wanted to try to make you happy. I thought this would make you happy again."

Joe started to calm down and replied, "I know doll. I am sorry. Now go wash your face and put some makeup on so you do not look so bad. Everyone will know that you have disobeyed me if they see that mark."

He went on to say, "You should be embarrassed and ashamed."

Joe repeated these words to me over and over. I should be embarrassed and ashamed—and I was.

The trip to visit Joe's sister went well, at least I thought. Joe seemed incredibly happy to see her, and they shared numerous intimate moments and tears together. One morning, I was up early and made coffee. Joe's sister and her husband were also awake and came into the kitchen. We exchanged good mornings, and I asked if I could make them coffee.

Joe's sister said, "We were hoping to catch you without Joe for a few minutes."

"Oh?" I questioned, "What's up?"

Joe's sister went on to explain to me that his previous marriage had not been such a happy one. I listened patiently. She told me that Joe had nearly destroyed the relationship due to his extravagant spending of money he did not have. She revealed that Joe lived large, but he could not afford this lifestyle.

"Well, he does have his retirement from his company, and as sad as it is, he has the inheritance from both your parents passing, as well as his previous wife." I commented.

She looked at me and said, "Hope, what are you talking about? He did not retire. He got fired from that company. He worked in the mailroom. He might have gotten money from his wife's death, but my parents did not have money, so there was no inheritance."

"Are you sure?" I questioned. "This is quite shocking to learn."

"Oh dear," she commented. "I am sorry, but you should know the truth about Joe. We are concerned for your safety also," she continued. "Has Joe ever been violent toward you?" she asked.

Her husband chimed in and said, "If he is, you contact us right away."

"No," I lied. "Yes, I will contact you if something happens."

About that time Joe walked into the kitchen. "What's going on in here?" he asked.

"Oh, just getting some coffee, love," I commented. "Can I get you a cup?"

"Sure, doll," he said as he eyed his sister.

"My sister has not been telling you stories about me, has she?" he continued.

I laughed and said, "Only the ones about your adventurous childhood."

He smiled, as I handed him his coffee. "So, what is the agenda today?" Joe asked.

"We are headed to do some hiking so wear some good shoes," piped in Joe's brother-in-law.

"Great," commented Joe. "Who planned this trip again?"

We all laughed, but I knew what Joe meant by that comment. He was not happy about visiting his sister. Now I knew the reason why. The rest of the trip was uneventful, and Joe made sure I was never alone with her the remainder of the trip. This was the first and last time I would ever see her.

NO FUN IN THE SUN

Joe was so angry about the visit to see his sister. He said the visit was a waste of time and that instead we should be on the beach! So I planned a beach trip to surprise him. I thought this might help with his anger. The surprise seemed to please Joe and change his mood somewhat. He still had his moments of anger but seemed to look forward to going. The beach trip was over a holiday weekend, so I had mentioned to Joe, it might be a fun time to just relax. He agreed.

Needless to say, the trip was not relaxing, at least not for me. The beach resort where we stayed was high atop a mountain that overlooked the ocean. It was beautiful. I enjoyed the view of the gorgeous landscape from our balcony and envisioned a romantic evening. However, seeing the sharp edges of the cliffs, Joe envisioned killing me by throwing me off the mountain. He commented that he could completely snuff out my life and be back home before anyone knew I was missing. He let out a deep, evil laugh and then looked at me as tears began to roll down my face.

"What?" he asked. "You cannot take a joke?"

I knew this was no joke. During this trip, I was careful not to do anything to provoke Joe further. I was walking on eggshells the entire time, praying that my very existence did not anger him. I thought of the question Joe's sister had asked me. I knew that violence was not new for Joe and he must have hurt others, probably previous girlfriends and maybe even his deceased wife.

A PREMONITION OF DEATH

We returned from the island trip without further incidences of violence or threats, but I was living a life of terror. I prayed it would get better. If only I could help Joe to see that his anger was the result of the grief over his wife's death, and perhaps, he could use more grief counseling as well. Whenever I mentioned this, he would always agree but never went back for any counseling.

The following Monday, I returned to work after the long weekend. I got a call from my daughter, Rachel, early that Monday morning. She was frantic.

"Thank God! Mom, are you okay?" Rachel asked as soon as I answered the phone.

"Yes," I said, "What is wrong?"

Rachel went on to explain that she had a terrible dream. No, not a dream, a nightmare that I had died. I assured her I was still very much alive. She could not be comforted as the nightmare really shook her up. I asked her to tell me about it. She explained that Joe was more controlling than ever and that she could not ever be alone with me. This was a common complaint from both her and Joshua.

I said, "Yes, you have mentioned this several times."

She told me that Joe had succeeded in completely isolating me from my family in her dream, and he had taken me away and no one knew where I was. In her dream, I had died, and Joe did not tell anyone. Joe planned my funeral, and there were no family members or friends there. She explained that she found out about this and went to Joe, who laughed at her and told her, "Your mom is already dead and buried, sorry."

She was clearly shaken up and made me promise to never go anywhere she did not know about, especially with Joe. She did not trust him. I promised her I would tell her, and then I assured her it was only a dream, and he would never do such things. All the while I knew he was fully capable of this atrocity. This seemed to calm her down, but looking back, this was not a dream or nightmare—it was a premonition.

CHAPTER 4

THE FINAL RECKONING

"I give them real and eternal life. They are protected from the Destroyer for good. No one can steal them from out of my hand. The Father who put them under my care is so much greater than the Destroyer and Thief. No one could ever get them away from him. I and the Father are one heart and mind."
John 10:28-30

I was disillusioned by how things turned out. I thought Joe and I would have the perfect life together. Instead, eveything had gone wrong it seemed. Somehow, I disappointed him and he became resentful toward me. He did not hold back his hatred either. I was not the person he thought I should be. He only saw ugliness in me and believed I was useless to him.

"A waste of space and air," he used to say, but he would not let me leave.

Even though I slept with a loaded gun pointed in my direction each night, Joe wanted to make sure I did not try to escape. Joe placed his numerous swords in front of the door, so if I opened it, there would be a terrible clanging noise to wake him up.

Joe regretted marrying me and did not hold back his feelings of annoyance and hatred for me. He would often tell me that I was not his savior but rather the thorn in his side. No one would ever compare with his deceased wife, and how did I even think I would ever measure up? I tried to explain to him that I respected her memory and the place she held in his heart, and I was not trying to replace her. Joe would hear none of it. I lived in a perpetual nightmare.

How did we get to this point? How could I continue to live like this? I thought I could make him happy. I did not want anyone to know what a huge mistake I had made, and now with his ongoing death threats to me and Joshua, it felt like there was no way out. All I could do was try my best to not cross him or make him angry. As I would soon learn, this was an insurmountable task.

THE SETUP

Our first wedding anniversary was coming soon, and I asked Joe if he would like to get away to celebrate. He did not feel this was a cause for celebration, but he reluctantly agreed. I saw this as something positive, and maybe we could reconcile our differences. I talked to Joe about my thoughts, as perhaps this could be a fresh start to our relationship. He seemed interested and agreed we needed a fresh start. This gave me hope that we could work things out. Joe was at least willing to talk about it, as there were still some times he seemed more like his old self, and we would have fun together. Joe would often lament about his behavior and did not understand why he acted like that at times. He would seem remorseful, but these times were less and less often. The mean and abusive side of Joe was becoming the norm.

Nonetheless, the plans were made for our first anniversary celebration and soon the day arrived. We flew into Reno and things were going splendidly. Joe seemed to be in good spirits. I was so thankful. We had an amazing dinner, and the evening could not have been better. I once again felt close to Joe. We stared into each others eyes and gooed over each other long after dinner had finished. It was like old times again, and it was hard to believe this was the same man that had such fits of anger.

The next day was wonderful, and it felt like the magic in our relationship was starting to come back. We went shopping and had a spectacular brunch. We enjoyed each other's company every minute of that day. I could only hope this was a new beginning. I shared with Joe my sentiments, and he agreed. He seemed so happy. Far from those dark thoughts that regularly overcame him.

We made plans later that afternoon to go to a comedy show with some new friends who lived in Reno. We had only met them a few times as they were friends with some of our other friends who lived near our hometown. These new friends had recently moved to Reno, so they were more than eager to have guests and entertain folks who came into town. They had planned the afternoon and evening events—a comedy show and dinner. Perfect. Since they were residents of Reno, they were able to get discounted show tickets and premier reservations at an exclusive restaurant. Even better.

I was excited to spend some time with our new friends, as every time we had been around them, Joe and I had so much fun. They seemed to really like Joe, and he liked them, so I thought this might put Joe in a better mood, as he did seem to be suffering from a bout of depression, lamenting again over his previous wife's death. I guess I could understand Joe's grief, but it was surprising that it seemed to consume him, and he refused to talk about it anymore. In the past, he always shared his feelings with me. Maybe I did not really understand since I have never lost a spouse or child.

During the comedy show we had several alcoholic drinks, and by the time the show had ended, we were all feeling in good humor. We laughed and talked with our new friends. It seemed like the perfect evening. Our friends picked a restaurant that was close by for dinner, but it was still a little early for our reservations, so we decided to go for more drinks at a local bar. According to our friends, this was a very popular spot for locals, and we would love it. The place was very nice, and we continued to laugh and talk. Joe seemed to be really enjoying himself, so I felt a little more relaxed about our situation.

As we got to know more about our friends, the conversation turned to politics and then religion. I remembered that our new friends were members of a church and had been involved in various activities, including the children's ministry. As the conversation started to get a bit hot and heavy on the political side, the husband stood up and announced that our reservation time was coming up soon. We summoned the waiter and paid our bill. Then, we shuffled out of the bar, Joe and I, arm in arm, down the street toward the restaurant.

NO DENIAL

Upon arrival at the restaurant, we were seated right away as we barely made our reservation time. The restaurant was exquisitely decorated, and we were seated at a circular table in a small alcove near the back of the restaurant. I excused myself to the ladies room while Joe and the others got comfortable at the table. When I returned, Joe had ordered drinks and wine. I told him I was feeling the other drinks quite a bit, but he was insistent that I not ruin the night and enjoy the evening. I smiled and agreed. He smiled back at me and again joined the conversation.

"Yes, Hope is one of those ridiculous people who I cannot convince otherwise," Joe chuckled. Both of our new friends started to laugh also.

"I must have missed something," I said sheepishly.

The wife started to explain that she no longer believed in God, that the concept of a god of the universe was a myth. Her husband agreed.

Joe continued, "I have tried to convince my senseless wife, but she still believes." They all laughed.

At that moment, I felt like I could not breathe, as if there was a noose around my neck.

"Come on Hope, don't be so naïve," the husband of our new friends said.

"Yes, she is really gullable and foolish for her beliefs," chimed in Joe. "I have tried to get her straightened out, but she refuses."

My new friends and husband continued to laugh at me for believing in God and started to taunt me and say how absurd I was for my beliefs.

"You are a smart woman with much education," the wife chimed in, "how can you believe in such nonsense?"

I was in shock, but even in my intoxicated state I would never renounce God, who had been so kind to me and spared my life on numerous occasions. Fortunately, the waiter came to the table to take our food order so that distracted the conversation to the menu.

"Stand up for me against world opinion and I'll stand up for you before my Father in heaven. If you turn tail and run, do you think I'll cover for you?"

MATTHEW 10:32-33

Looking back, I believe this was the point when the Lord said He had enough of this, and He was going to get me out of this situation. I would certainly suffer, but at least I would be out.

After we ordered our food, the subject changed to another topic, thankfully, and soon our friends and Joe were in a debate about world government. All taunting and teasing of my beliefs were forgotten, for now, but I did not forget. After finishing dinner and drinks, we decided to share a cab that would return us to our hotel and then take our friends back home as they did not live far from where we were staying.

I sat in the back of the cab between Joe and the wife of our new friends. The husband sat in the front seat with the driver. We chatted on the way to our hotel. Everything seemed to be going well, except the mention of not believing in God as I knew this was a trigger point for Joe, but he seemed to have forgotten the conversation.

ALCOHOL-INDUCED HATRED

We paid our portion of the cab fair and wished our friends a good evening. As we walked to our room, a drunk man whistled at me or someone, I was not really paying too much attention, but Joe was. Once the drunk man was out of sight, Joe grabbed my arm and told me I would pay for this.

"How could you have tried to cheat on me, right there in front of me, on our anniversary?" he steamed under his breath. "You are nothing but a wretched whore. Why would anyone want you? I sure don't."

Even though I was intoxicated, I could feel the anger and hatred growing inside of him. I knew I was going to be beaten if not killed by him. I tried to explain that I did not realize that man was even whistling at me, and I did not even look at him or know what was going on. But that did not convince Joe. His anger flared beyond measure. I carried the bags from our day of shopping and continued to walk through the casino. Joe pushed me into the elevator. I knew my fate as we rode up the elevator.

The door opened, and Joe declared, "You better not try to run away, or you will suffer a fate worse than death."

He opened the door to our room, and I prayed.

DEFEATED OR SO IT SEEMED

Once we were in the hotel room, Joe unleashed his rage on me for the last time. He knocked me down, and I got up and ran to the bathroom. He followed, and as I tried to escape, he grabbed me and pelted me so hard over and over on the side of my face, I fell to the ground.

"GET UP!" he screamed.

I did my best to get up, and as soon as I was, a crushing blow came across my face, and I fell into the vanity, hitting my head. I fought consciousness because I knew if I lost this, I would die. I stood up and looked in the mirror. Blood was streaming from my nose and mouth, and there was a large knot growing on my forehead where I had hit the vanity.

"TRY TO CHEAT ON ME AGAIN, YOU WHORE!" Joe yelled, as I ran out of the bathroom into the bedroom.

Joe jumped on me, and I fell to the floor. He turned me over and sat on top of me. I knew this was the end as I felt his hands around my neck. I tried to get away and managed to get his hands off my neck. Joe lifted my arms and held them as he delivered blow after blow to my abdomen, then moved on to finish me off by punching me in the face. The once intense pain started to fade as I lost consciousness. I tried to stay awake, but I could no longer hold on. My last conscious thought was that I would see Jesus soon.

Once I was unconscious, Joe must have stopped beating me and taken all of my clothes off and placed me on the bed. I have no recollection of it. He must have thought I was dead or that he was tired and would finish me off and dispose of my body in the morning. After all, I had been suffering from this terrible unknown autoimmune illness that was well documented, so it would not be unexpected that I would randomly die, or better yet, he would say I just ran off somewhere, or someone kidnapped me. He could come up with a great story in the morning. Joe drifted off peacefully to sleep as I lay there by his side, naked, unconscious, and bleeding.

"God keeps an eye on his friends, his ears pick up every moan and groan."

PSALM 34:15

Suddenly, there was a knock on the door. Was I dreaming? No, not a knock, a pounding! Maybe it was my head? No, it was definitely a pounding on the door. I could not move as I was still in a state of semi-consciousness. The pounding continued for what seemed like hours before I heard a voice yell out, and then I thought I saw Joe jump out of bed. Was I dreaming? Had I died?

"In trouble, deep trouble, I prayed to GOD. He answered me.
From the belly of the grave I cried, 'Help!' You heard my cry."

JONAH 2:2

THE FINAL RECKONING

"POLICE, OPEN UP, NOW!"

There was no mistaking those words. Joe told me to stay in bed and not to say a word. When he opened the door, he was immediately taken down and handcuffed. It is a little hard to remember the specific order of the details of what happened next, but all of a sudden, Joe was gone. He was taken out of the room in handcuffs. A security guard came and got me out of bed and gave me a robe.

"What happened?" he asked.

I could hear Joe yelling that I better stay quiet, but the security guard said, "He cannot hurt you anymore. We will get you to a hospital. Call 911!"

"No," I cried. "Joe has people at the hospital, and he will contact them to kill me. He has told me this."

The security guard smiled assuringly at me and asked if I would talk to the police. He explained that Joe was going to jail whether I filed charges against him or not. It was the state law. Even though I was terrified, I agreed to talk to the police. I could hardly stand when the police entered my room, and they immediately told me they needed to call an ambulance.

"No," I cried in protest, "he has people who he will contact in the hospital who will kill me. I just need to get out of here."

The policeman told me I was safe, and they would not let him get to me.

"Can you talk to us and tell us what happened?" one of the officers asked.

"Yes, I think so," I said.

I explained to them what I could remember of the assault, even though I felt as if I was going in and out of consciousness. The officer again told me I needed to go to the emergency room for the treatment of my injuries, as I likely had a concussion. I again refused. This was my one chance to get out. If I did not take it now, I would certainly end up dead. I knew, despite my semi-conscious state, that God sent his angels to protect me. Somewhere, somehow, there were angels around, and the police were called to try to stop the beating.

> "Evil can't get close to you, harm can't get through the door. He ordered his angels to guard you wherever you go. If you stumble, they'll catch you; their job is to keep you from falling."
>
> PSALM 91:10-12

I finished my statement to the police officer, who gave me a copy of the report that he would file. The security guard gathered Joe's belongings and told me he could pick them up when he was released from jail and that I should not worry about them. I did not know where they were taking his belongings, but it did not seem to matter at that point. I was confused and in severe pain.

A member of the hotel staff came to the room to help move me to another secured room on another floor. There was a security guard posted outside my doorway in case Joe got out of jail before I was able to leave. I knew I had to get away before he was released from jail because there was now no doubt in my mind that he would kill me. The police officer who took my statement told me that they would hold Joe in jail for at least twelve hours.

"Get some rest now," he said, "and then head to the airport in the morning. If you decide you need to go to the hospital, there will be an officer outside your room."

I thanked everyone for their help and then laid in bed. The room was spinning, and I did not know if it was because of the concussion, the alcohol, or both. All I knew is that I had my chance to get out of this nightmare over the next twelve hours, and although I was terrified, I was not going to let this opportunity slip away.

JESUS IS CALLING US TO FREEDOM

As I look back on that fateful day, I realized that Jesus called me out of bondage into freedom. Although I was battered and beaten, Jesus was faithful and got me out of that situation. Jesus said that no one can snatch us out of His hands (John 10:29). Not only did Jesus protect me from being stolen out of his hands by Satan that day, but He also continually pursued and protected me to bring me back into the fold when I went astray all those months back.

Now, I can relate my deliverance to the parable of the lost sheep, where Jesus taught, "Look at it this way. If someone has a hundred sheep and one of them wanders off, doesn't he leave the ninety-nine and go after the one?" (Matthew 18:12). These words have rung loud and clear to me since that day. I believe I was the one that day who Jesus would not let go of.

It is not God's will for us to live in bondage. This not only includes physical bondage, but the bondage of emotional, spiritual, or mental abuse. The freedom Jesus offers all of us includes being free of fear, anxiety, bad thoughts, substance abuse, and other manifestations that accompany domestic violence. As Christians, we know our freedom was paid for with a hefty price at the cross. Jesus died to free us from our sins that enslave us. In His death, we are now free from sin ruling and controlling our lives.

I would add that this is true not only for our sin but also for the sin of others, especially in the case of domestic abuse or violence. In Luke 4:18, Jesus quotes from Isaiah that He was sent to proclaim freedom for the prisoners and to set the oppressed free. But to be in true freedom, we must leave our old life behind and start a new life. We cannot be freed and then return right back to the life we were living. This does not mean that we will not slip up from time to time, but it does mean that we can be forgiven as we continue to walk by faith and have a relationship with Jesus Christ.

Being free does not give us the right to do whatever we want, whenever we want, but true freedom no longer allows fear or anxiety to rule our lives. Only Jesus can offer this freedom as His sovereignty reigns over our lives and gives us a peace and joy that others do not understand.

Please do not make the mistakes I did. Come back into the fold. Jesus is calling you back!

> "Christ has set us free to live a free life. So take your stand! Never again let anyone put a harness of slavery on you."
>
> GALATIANS 5:1

CHAPTER 5

THE AFTERSHOCK

An aftershock is an aftereffect of a distressing or traumatic event.[3] Aftereffects or delayed effects can be equally traumatizing following the main event. I cannot lie to you about this. Mine were harrowing, but somehow, only by the grace of God, I survived. This is a critical point in domestic abuse, as the abuser is usually remorseful for what they have done and wants the abused person to return to them. But if they do not, then get ready, as most abusers (who I would classify also as narcissists) will not take no for an answer. These abusers want their way no matter what, and you must do as they say or else. So they believe.

"And that about wraps it up. God is strong, and he wants you strong. So take everything the Master has set out for you, well-made weapons of the best materials. And put them to use so you will be able to stand up to everything the Devil throws your way. This is no weekend war that we'll walk away from and forget

> about in a couple of hours. This is for keeps, a life-or-death fight
> to the finish against the Devil and all his angels."
>
> EPHESIANS 6:10-12

THE MORNING AFTER

As the morning dawned it seemed like a dream. This could not have happened, or did it? I was in the room the hotel personnel moved me to the previous night where I slept on and off but sobered up. I knew I had to get out as soon as I could. I called the airlines and got a reservation for an earlier flight. Then I called my children to tell them what had happened. My two sons, Caleb and Joshua, agreed to meet me and pick me up at the airport, and then they would help me get my stuff from my apartment, and I would be able to go home with Caleb or stay in a hotel.

It was not quite a plan, but I thought it would work out. I also called my parents to tell them, and they were very upset. I was not sure what to do, but I got my belongings packed up the best I could and checked out of the hotel.

I looked in the mirror and did not even recognize myself. I had a huge knot on my forehead and both my eyes were black and swollen. I could barely see out of them. There was a large bruise around my mouth that went up to the left side of my nose. My hand was hurting, and any movement caused significant pain. My ribs were hurting, and I could barely walk, but I knew I had to get away and get to safety before they let Joe out of jail, or he would kill me.

The fear inside of me would not subside, and I felt an increased urgency to get out of there as soon as possible. I knew I looked awful, but I did the best I could to try to disguise the injuries to my face. I summoned all my courage and checked out of the hotel and took a cab to the airport. I had no clue of Joe's fate or if he would be released and follow me to the airport. Would I run into him at the airport? Would he kill me on the spot if he saw me? I think I knew the answer to this question, but I had to keep going.

Once I was on the airplane, I relaxed just a little bit. The pain was overwhelming, and I thought I might pass out, but I knew I had to get home. Luckily, no one on the airplane talked to me, although people stared. I did not care if they stared at me or not; I just wanted to go home and be done with this crazy situation. I knew my life was still in great danger, but I did not know what else to do at this point. I guess I would be able to figure that out once I got home and everyone knew the truth about Joe.

HOME

When I got off the airplane, Caleb and Joshua were waiting. They insisted that I go to the emergency room, where I could be treated for my injuries. I was so distraught, given the trauma I had just undergone, that all I wanted to do was get a few things and get away from the area, as I knew Joe would be back to finish off what he started. I finally agreed that perhaps I would go to an urgent care facility just for a quick check-up to make sure that I did not have any internal bleeding or severe injuries. I was briefly checked out at an urgent care facility, and after about an hour, I agreed to follow up in the emergency room if I had any ongoing symptoms conducive to trauma. I had broken ribs and possibly suffered a concussion but seemed to be functional at this point, so I was given a prescription for pain medication and sent on my way.

Once Joe was out of jail, he sent horrible, threatening text and voicemail messages to me. He did not know the airlines we flew on or how to get home. I probably should have not responded to his threatening text messages and voicemails, but I was terrified and did not know what to do. Joshua was able to communicate to him the flight information that he would need at the airport. Joe had access to my bank account, so he was able to see the charges of the hotel where we decided to stay. He threatened to kill anyone who helped me, including members of my family.

Joe had been able to view me coming into the apartment to gather a few things, but when we entered, we covered the cameras that Joe had installed to watch my every move. Thankfully, he was not able to see who helped me. I gathered the dogs and took them with me as the pet sitter was no longer scheduled to come to feed them, and I did not know how long Joe would be in returning. Joe demanded that I bring the dogs back to the apartment once he knew I had taken them. Joshua agreed to meet Joe to provide a key to the apartment as Joe's keys (including his car keys) were in the lost and found at the hotel along with his other personal effects. Somehow, when he went back to the hotel, he did not ask for these items. He demanded I contact the hotel and have them sent overnight to him. I did this as I was terrified of what the repercussions might be if I did not.

I stayed with Caleb's family for a short while as the tirades of text messages and voicemails from Joe continued. There were times when he would try to ping my phone to find out where I was staying. I was frightened, not only for me but for Caleb's family as they were hiding me. How could I have been so gullible and naïve by bringing this terrible monster into my family's life? The guilt and terror were paralyzing.

I managed to remove his access to my bank accounts and credit cards. I changed my passwords on my emails and other accounts, so he could no longer have access to these. This infuriated him, and he became increasingly threatening to me. Finally, I had enough and blocked his number. Joe could no longer contact me or make threats to me, but it was terrifying all the same as I did not know what his next move would be.

Rachel had moved recently, so I decided to go and stay with her for a little while. During my stay with Rachel, I unblocked Joe's number. There were numerous text and voicemails that immediately downloaded where Joe was apologetic. He told me in the text messages that the "Being" had taken over his mind and body, and he had no idea what had happened. He had blacked out, and the next thing he knew he awoke in jail. When he demanded to know where his wife was, the police officers explained that he had beaten me and had been arrested. They chalked it up to another drunken offense so often seen in this town.

He begged me to contact him to let him know that I was all right and not seriously hurt. He knew I must have been somewhat coherent as he had received his belongings from the hotel. He texted that the whole thing seemed like a blur, and he could not remember even coming back home. He had a vague idea of what had transpired but only from the details of the police officers. Joe begged me to meet with him to talk through things. He wanted to see if there was any way to patch things up between us. He begged me to come home, so he could care for my wounds he had inflicted. He promised that nothing like this would ever happen again, but I knew he was a liar.

COME BACK OR ELSE!

Ultimately, I had to return to the area where I lived as my wounds were healed, and I had to return to work. I was terrified as to what Joe might do, but at the moment, we seemed to be on good terms, given the circumstances. Despite my family's concerns, I agreed to meet Joe in a public place—a coffee shop near our home. It was warm, so he brought the dogs, and we sat outside and talked while we drank our coffee. Joe claimed to have no recollection of the assault and did not know why he woke up in jail. Of course, he now knew the whole story, and he seemed shocked and appalled. Joe begged me to come home.

I told him we needed time to see if we could salvage the marriage, and I needed time to heal emotionally. I arranged to move to another apartment complex (but I did not tell Joe the location) and planned to move mine and Joshua's belongings there in about a week. I told Joe that I would need access to our home as he had the locks changed when he returned from Reno. As much as Joe begged and pleaded, I told him I needed time away to sort this all out.

Joe finally commented that he knew himself, and this time was too long for him to wait. He would need to move on. I told him I was sorry that was the case, and if he needed to move on then I suppose it was not meant to be. As we fought back the tears, Joe told me he was sorry for what he had done. I forgave him and told him I hoped we could put this behind us and move on in time. He smiled and told me he had brought me a few of my things. As he walked to the car to get them, I knew we would never be together again. Joe would move on quickly, and I would just be left with the memories.

Once I felt recovered from my injuries, I returned to work. On my first day back, Joe reached out to me and asked me to have dinner with him.

I was a little hesitant, but he told me he had something important to tell me. I reluctantly agreed to meet him at a local sandwich shop that evening. As the day passed, I focused on my work but could not help but wonder what Joe needed to tell me. It sounded urgent.

After work, I met Joe at the sandwich shop. He seemed a little anxious, and I asked if everything was okay.

He smiled and said, "I hope so."

Joe then proceeded to tell me a wild story of how he got out of jail in Reno. He then asked me if I remembered when he told me that he had been hired to do some work for a government agency a while back. I told him I remembered, but I was not aware of the type of work he had done. He then told me an elaborate story of how he had been hired as a hitman to track down criminals who escaped justice. He then claimed to have called this agency in Reno to get him out of jail, but for them to do this, he would be required to return the favor, so to speak. I could not believe what I was hearing.

Joe went on to describe how he had been approached by a tall brunette while grocery shopping that day, who told him he would soon be given his mission. She also questioned why his wife had moved out of the home as this was a red flag to the agency. Joe went on to describe that they were suspicious that he was going to rescind his promise to do a job for them. The agency saw my moving out as a sign that he was going to try to escape.

Joe went on to tell me to be careful as the agency had people following me. I asked Joe if he could just pay the money back owed for the bail, and he explained that it was not that simple as they had paid off a judge to release him. This all sounded crazy to me, but Joe had told me stories before of how he had people in the agency who were able to do background checks on me and provide him details of all my text messages and phone conversations.

Over the months before the assault, Joe produced what seemed like legitimate papers of his connection to this agency. I was frightened and did not know what to do. Joe explained that I must come home, so they would not get suspicious. Joe warned me that I would be kidnapped, tortured, and killed if I did not come back home. I was terrified as Joe described what types of things this agency would do to me.

"Hope, I am only trying to protect you. You need to come back home or else the agency will find you and kill you," Joe frantically explained.

I decided to take my chances. *Either way, I was going to end up dead*, I thought to myself, *but it would not be at the hands of Joe.*

ESCALATED THREATS

The following evening, as I was trying to unpack, I received a frantic phone call from Joe. He told me I must escape my apartment right now as they were coming for me. I was terrified!

"What do I do?" I asked Joe.

Joe told me to grab a few items of clothing and anything else I would need to stay the night as he promised to protect me. Joshua was out of town, and I did not know what to do, so I did as Joe said. I packed a few items that I would need to go to work the next day and then headed over to our old home to meet Joe.

As I drove, Joe talked to me on the phone. He insisted on keeping me on the line as he thought I might be picked off any moment. I looked down, and I saw that my trunk was open.

"Oh no!" I cried.

Joe said, "Whatever you do, don't stop."

I drove to the old apartment, terrified that I had seen my last day on earth. Joe instructed me to drive up the parking garage and to park one level up. I did as he asked, and he met me in the parking garage. He had a gun with a silencer on it and told me to hurry inside. When I walked inside the apartment, Joe had guns laid out everywhere. There were automatic weapons set up on stands that pointed to the outside windows, and all the blinds were closed.

"Quick," Joe exclaimed. "Stay down."

I obeyed his words as I could tell he was frightened and wanted to protect me. Joe hugged me, and said, "You are safe now."

I expressed my gratitude to him, and he said, "Well it is not over, but at least you are safe for now."

Joe instructed me that I should act normal at my job tomorrow and not tell anyone about this. He warned me that the agency he was working with was part of the FBI, and if I mentioned anything to anyone, we would both be killed.

"They do not leave loose ends," he cautioned.

I was terrified and agreed to follow his instructions. I was so exhausted as I had not slept for days now due to the terror, which was my life once again. I begged Joe to pray with me, and he looked at me and laughed, "Your God cannot save you now!"

I began to cry. He told me he would not let anything happen to me as he was now my god and that I should get rest. He would stay up all night and keep watch. I was so exhausted that I could not help but agree on getting rest. I laid my head down and dozed off for a few hours. When I awoke, Joe was looking out the window.

"Everything okay?" I asked.

Joe did not reply.

As morning approached, I started to get ready to go to work. Joe seemed angry that I fell asleep while he stood watch.

"How could you sleep when I needed you?" he yelled.

As his anger grew, I realized that I must get out of there.

"I am sorry," I cried. "I was just so exhausted as I have not slept in days. I will leave and go to work now. Thank you for watching out for me," I added.

"Yes, you need to get to work," Joe mumbled.

I quickly got dressed and gathered my belongings and started to head for the door. Joe grabbed my hand and ripped off my wedding ring. "You won't be needing this anymore," he yelled. "Get out!"

I ran out the door, not knowing what had enraged him so much. I knew that it was not over yet, and I would have to deal with Joe again, but I would take my chances with the agency, I supposed. There was nowhere to run or escape.

Once I got to work, I relaxed just a bit, but then the text messages and phone calls from Joe started up again. I tried my best to work without anyone noticing that I was on the phone. By mid-morning, the threats had escalated to a whole new level. It was that moment that I decided I could not do this on my own. I needed help. I prayed to God that I would do the right thing, and that if I died, He would forgive me.

I walked down to the third floor of the office building and my friend and co-worker, Mike Fuller, was in his office. Mike saw me and motioned for me to come in. He could see I was quite distraught and told me to shut the door. Mike, who oversaw security for the United States operations at my company and was a former FBI agent, sat in amazement as I told him the whole story.

"Hope, I had no idea you were going through such a terrifying situation. You came to the right person," Mike smiled.

I trusted him, so I knew he would help me.

"First," Mike said, "Let me assure you that the FBI does not have 'an agency' of hitmen as Joe has described. There is no secret undercover group such as this. Let me call a friend of mine who is still with the FBI, and we can get to the bottom of Joe's claims right away. I want to be assured he is not associated with an organized crime group," he added. "Meanwhile, I will check into a few options regarding your personal safety and get back to you."

"Thank you so much," I told Mike. "I do appreciate it."

When I returned to my desk, I had more than thirty voicemails and text messages from Joe. I was terrified. I tried to focus on my work, but it was impossible. I knew that Joe would not be silent, but I did not know what he would do next. As the hours waned, the messages became more hostile, and the threats of violence escalated. Joe told me he was no longer going to tolerate my disobedience to him, and he was going to act.

Again, Joe threatened to bring me the heads of my grandchildren as a punishment, but it was too late for me to turn back now. I think at this point Joe realized he was losing the battle, but he would not give up. After the last threat, I returned to Mike's office, but he was not there. I called Mike's mobile number, and he told me to go into his office and wait for him. After what seemed like an eternity, Mike returned and gave me information on what I needed to do to file an order of protection against Joe. I told Mike that I would do this but that he should listen to the voice messages. Mike listened in horror.

As if right on cue, the messages ended, and Mike's phone rang.

"I will be right there," I heard Mike say.

Mike told me to sit tight in his office and not to leave. He would be right back. I saw Mike go to the office next to his and summon the assistant director of security. They both exited the area quickly, and all I could do was sit and wait.

Joe had come to my office to look for me. Fortunately, Mike already alerted the security guard on duty of the situation, so he would not let Joe into the building. Instead, he was to call him. Mike and the assistant director confronted Joe and asked him to leave the premises, or they would call the police. Joe did not make a scene and left without incident.

On the way out, Joe ran into a friend of ours. She had no idea what was going on. Joe told her he had dropped off something for me, and we were going to meet up later, as if there was nothing wrong. She later confided in me that she had gone to meet friends after work and on her way home had stopped for gas. Joe was at the same gas station filling up his car. She commented that she thought it was unusual for him to be on that side of town, but he was alone, so she did not say anything to him nor did he see her. That gas station happened to be across the street from my new apartment. He was in pursuit.

I had no idea this was going on until I received a text and voice message from Joe stating that this was my last chance to leave and join him. He told me that the former FBI agent and his sidekick would be killed as well as anyone else who helped me.

"If you care anything about them, you will leave and meet me now," he demanded.

It was too late for that now. The jig is up Joe, and you have been busted! Mike returned and told me what had happened.

"Do not worry," Mike said. "We have a plan. Just sit tight."

I fully trusted Mike and knew that I would never have to deal with Joe one-on-one again. People knew what was going on now.

MY HIDING PLACE

That evening, my work arranged for me to go stay at a safe house miles away. My car was hidden, and I was given a private phone that no one knew the number. I was instructed to only give this number to my family so they could communicate with me. For my safety, I was to turn my phone off and leave it in my office, so Joe could not track me. Mike accompanied me to my apartment in an unmarked car to obtain some of my belongings. I quickly gathered some things together and returned to the unmarked car that would take me to an undisclosed location. I could not believe this was happening to me. Mike informed me that he heard back from his friend at the FBI. Joe was not part of organized crime and in fact used his own credit card to get out of jail in Reno. Joe was a liar—a dangerous and deranged liar.

When I arrived at the safe house, the lady who owned it showed me to my room. I used the phone to call my family to give them the new number and to explain what had happened. After I completed my calls, the lady knocked on the door and said, "Why don't you come down and let me fix you some tea. We can talk if you want."

It was late, but I accepted the offer and told her my story. She did not seem shocked or surprised but was comforting. She reassured me that I was safe here. I thanked her repeatedly for her kindness, but her only comment was that one day, I could pay it forward. Following the tea, I retired to my room. The lady told me I could stay as long as I liked. I knew I would have to be bold and take the steps I needed to get away from Joe for good, but that could wait until the morning. I finally laid my head down and got rest for the first time in weeks.

It was clear that my life was going to change forever now. I was in a hiding place to prevent my husband from killing me. It was hard to imagine any situation that could be worse. Thank God, Joshua was still out of town. He had not returned to our home with Joe since the assault. He gathered up the things he needed and was already scheduled to go on vacation during the weeks following the assault, but he would be returning soon.

During this time, I had to move all of Joshua's and my belongings to our new place on my own. I had movers help with the big stuff like furniture. Joe gave me a few things like a bed frame but no mattress. Ironically, the mattress was actually mine. Joe also packed up a bunch of belongings from his previous marriage and sent them with the movers as well. I donated these items to charity because I for sure did not want them. It was strange because right after I moved my few belongings (and while Joshua was still gone) is when Joe stalked me at work. I had been hiding out with friends or at the safe house but knew I would have to move forward at our new apartment at some point as I could not stay hidden forever.

THE BATTLE FOR FREEDOM BEGINS

The lady who I stayed with was gone by the time I got up the next morning. When I walked downstairs, her husband asked me if I wanted breakfast.

"Sure," I said, "but I have not had much luck at eating lately with all the stress, so please do not be offended if I do not eat much."

"How about a smoothie?" he asked.

"That sounds great," I said.

As I drank the smoothie, he asked me what I needed from him. "I am happy to drive you wherever you need to go," he said. "You know you are welcome to stay here as long as you like," he smiled.

"Let me call my attorney," I replied, "and maybe you could drop me off at his office?"

"Sure," he replied. "No problem."

I called the attorney I used for my previous divorce years back as I did not know who else to call. It just so happened that when I dialed his office, his wife answered the phone. I had remembered her from all those years back. Both she and her husband were Christians and were a help to me previously. I told her who I was, and she seemed to remember me as well. I relayed a little of my story to her and told her I was not quite sure what I needed to do, but I thought I might need a restraining order and a divorce. She explained that I could get an order of protection, which was much stricter than a restraining order, and suggested I come to the office that afternoon. I agreed that I would be there in the afternoon to get the ball rolling. I was praying that I could get this order of protection today, so I could at least feel a little bit safer.

She scheduled an appointment for me, and I thanked her. I returned to tell my plans to my host.

"Happy to help," he said.

I turned to him with tears in my eyes. I said, "I don't know how or when I could ever repay you."

He smiled and told me that one day I would repay, as he knew I would pay it forward to someone else who needed help. *What an amazing example of kindness*, I thought. I will never forget what these people did to help me. I am eternally grateful for their help and all the assistance from my workplace. I am not sure what would have happened to me if they would not have stepped in.

I arrived at my attorney's office at the appointed time. Fortunately, my attorney had been able to clear his schedule for the afternoon, so I had his undivided attention. I told him my tale of horror, including all the demonic experiences with the "Being." I told him all the threats to kill me and my son as well as my other children. I had pictures of the beating I sustained in Reno, as well as the court documents that testified to the life I lived with Joe. My attorney listened in amazement. Although he believed what I was telling him, I am not quite sure he had ever heard such a wild tale.

"The first thing we need to do," he exclaimed, "is to get an emergency order of protection against Joe."

"Won't this make him angry?" I asked.

"Probably," said my attorney, "but better for him to be angry and be sitting in jail if he tries to come after you then having no consequences."

My attorney got busy completing the forms. It seemed like he asked me thousands of questions, but I am sure it was only four or five. He asked his wife to type up information, and we worked for what felt like hours to get this prepared. My attorney told me to stay at his office, and he would go to the court and file the paperwork.

"By the way," he commented as he walked out the door, "I am also going to file the divorce papers so the judge will see you mean business."

Wow, I thought to myself. *This is really happening.*

Once my attorney returned, he gave me copies of the papers he filed.

"All we need to do now is wait for the judge to grant the emergency protection order," my attorney explained.

"How long will that take?" I asked.

"Depends," he said, "usually a couple of days. I did ask the clerk to consider that this case was an emergency, so we will see." He went on to explain, "From there, assuming the judge grants the emergency order of protection, Joe will have to be served, so he is aware of the proceedings. In this case, Joe will be served with the emergency order of protection as well as the divorce papers. It will be a double whammy for him."

I was worried, knowing Joe would be angry and go into a rage when this happened.

"Do not worry," my attorney said, "you will be protected on the day this happens."

I smiled but was still nervous about the entire process. *I hope Joshua will be back by then*, I thought to myself. *I could really use his support about now.*

I called Mike back at my office. He agreed to come and pick me up at my attorney's office and drop me off at a rental car location.

"We have your car hidden," he explained, "so no one knows where it is. Joe will never find it and will not know what you are driving."

"Thank you so much," I said. "I don't know what I would have done without your help."

Mike just smiled. I decided to rent a car so that Joe would not recognize what I was driving. I was escorted by an undercover security guard from my company for days when I returned to work. I was overcome with gratitude but at the same time felt unbelievable shame knowing that my colleagues knew what a terrible mistake I had made marrying Joe. When I returned, the executive director of my company even paid a visit to me in my office to let me know how supportive he would be if I needed to work from an undisclosed location or needed time off. He commented that when he heard the story, as he needed to be informed due to the security issue, he was shocked to find out it was me they were talking about.

"You were the last person who came to my mind when I heard this horrible story, Hope," he said. "I would have never believed it."

I smiled and said, "Yes, sadly, it is me," while the shame welled up inside. It was all I could do to hold back the tears.

I had not heard from Joe since the incident at my work. He had plenty of legal problems to deal with as he was required to return to Reno for a hearing on his assault charge. My attorney contacted the courts in Reno to find out the date of his hearing, but there was no need for that as Joe posted all over social media that he was headed back to Reno and had taken photos with a celebrity he saw at the airport.

"I am glad he was so choked up over the marriage ending," my attorney chuckled.

Joe was making a mockery of the court system. Shortly after I had heard of the celebrity picture postings on social media, I got word that the judge granted my emergency order of protection. Joe would be served with this order as well as the divorce papers within the next few days.

Meanwhile, after Joe returned from Reno, he sent me an email apologizing for his behavior. He mourned everything that happened, especially the assault and coming to my work. He promised me he would leave me and my family alone. I sent this to my attorney to ask if we should drop the order of protection.

My attorney chuckled, "Are you out of your mind, Hope?"

Maybe, I thought. I just wanted Joe to leave me and my family alone.

"We are going through with this," my attorney said. "A police officer is on his way to deliver the news. I will let you know how it goes. I am sure the officer will be in touch with one of us once he delivers the papers."

Within an hour of this conversation with my attorney, I received a call from the officer who delivered the order of protection and divorce papers to Joe. He told me it took several attempts to deliver the papers, but he finally caught Joe at home. Joe seemed in good spirits when he answered the door and did not seem surprised. The officer explained the contents of both sets of papers to Joe. Joe thanked the officer for his trouble and assured him he would obey the order of protection and stay as far away from me as he possibly could. I was relieved at this because previously Joe begged me to send the police to him. Joe threatened to "take no prisoners" if any police came to his door and that they would have to kill him first. In other words, Joe was threatening "suicide by cop."

ORDER OF PROTECTION HEARING

My attorney explained that there would be a hearing with a judge to have the order of protection made into a permanent order. This meant I would have to go before the judge and testify about what Joe did to me and the threats he made. My attorney told me to bring the pictures of my injuries, as well as copies of the threatening voicemails, text messages, and emails. I would be required to testify in front of Joe and his attorney. Joe's attorney would also get to cross examine me as part of Joe's defense. My attorney explained that having an order of protection against you is not a good situation as it shows up on an employment background check. We both knew Joe would soon need a job unless he found a woman that he could manipulate to support him. Even though it had been less than a month since the assault, Joe was already on the prowl. He joined a local singles group and posted pictures on social media of himself and his new conquests.

I dreaded the day of the hearing, but I had to go through with it. I met my attorney at the courthouse alone with no support from family or friends. My attorney and I entered the courtroom and were seated. Joe and his attorney were making small talk about traveling to the south of France for vacation all while I thought I might hurl at any moment from nerves. Joe's smugness and cockiness were evident, which was even more sickening to me. What did I ever see in him? I prayed to God for His help; I certainly needed it that day.

I was on the witness stand for five hours. Joe thought he would be cool and interrupt my attorney when he wanted, which made the judge burn with anger. Finally, the judge threatened for Joe to be quiet, or she would find him in contempt and throw him in jail.

I was not prepared for what Joe's attorney was going to throw out at me. First, he asked me if I was a prostitute.

"No," I answered.

"Isn't your side business just a cover for an escort service?" he added as if he had not heard my answer of no.

"No," I said again.

"Aren't you a stripper?" he continued.

I did not answer as Joe's attorney continued to berate and badger me. He told the judge I suffered from a dissociative personality disorder and that I was a threat to myself and society. Joe was a hero in that he intervened to protect and save me from hurting myself and others. If it got a little rough, then Joe apologized, but it was necessary to prevent me from doing myself any more harm. He accused me of inflicting these wounds on myself. Furthermore, Joe's attorney claimed encounters with the "Being" were a sexual fantasy game we used to play. I was overwhelmed and thought I might become sick or faint.

At this point, the judge interrupted and said in a loud voice, "I do not care if she is a prostitute, stripper, or has two hundred personalities. This is irrelevant to the case. No one deserves to be beaten in this manner, and I do not think for one moment that she did this to herself. I just want to know if this man committed this violent act to her and in the future, if he will continue to be a threat to her."

At this point, Joe's attorney said he was finished with his line of questioning. Thank you, JESUS! I was about to have a breakdown.

"At my preliminary hearing no one stood by me. They all ran like scared rabbits. But it doesn't matter—the Master stood by me and helped me spread the Message loud and clear to those who had never heard it. I was snatched from the jaws of the lion! God's looking after me, keeping me safe in the kingdom of heaven. All praise to him, praise forever! Oh, yes!"

2 TIMOTHY 4:16-18

Then, it was my attorney's turn to go at Joe and go at him, he did.

"So, Joe, what you are saying is that the vanity reached up and slapped Hope in the head? Are you saying that she could not stand up, yet she was able to carry the bags from the days shopping excursion to the room? Which is it?" my attorney pelted.

Then there was the matter of my belongings. Joe told the judge he would not give me any of my belongings, primarily my clothing because he wanted to sell them to recoup his losses. This infuriated the judge!

She snapped at Joe, "What are you a cross-dresser? Give this girl back all her clothing! And if you sold anything, you either get it back or pay her the difference. Do you understand?"

You would have thought that Joe and his attorney would have taken a hint that things were not going too well for them, but then they started to argue with the judge. At this moment, she excused herself and said she would be back momentarily with a decision. The judge returned in minutes and told us she had reached a verdict. She believed that Joe had caused physical harm and that he was an ongoing threat to me, so she granted the permanent order of protection. Thank you, Lord!

Of course, Joe had questions and used this as an opportunity to smart talk to the judge. He mouthed off, "What if we are at the same place? I am not leaving if she shows up."

I think this was the last straw for the judge.

"Figure it out," she yelled.

"Young lady," she called to me, "please approach the bench."

"Yes, ma'am," I said as I walked forward.

"Do not make a mockery of this court. I have granted this decision because I believe you. This man is a menace, and I expect you to stay clear of him. Do you understand me?"

"Yes ma'am, you do not need to worry about that," I replied. "I have no intention of ever being around this man again."

"Good," the judge said, "you are way too good for him anyway."

I could see Joe burning with anger as he left the courtroom.

> "First pride, then the crash—
> the bigger the ego, the harder the fall."
>
> PROVERBS 16:18

Overall, we had been in the courtroom almost eight hours that day under very intense circumstances. I was grateful that at least this part was over, but I knew this was just the beginning of a lengthy battle. One that would last longer than the sham that was our marriage.

IT IS NOT OVER YET

Following the assault and Joe's arrest in Reno, I learned that he paid his bail of $3,000.00. Since my attorney wasn't licensed in Nevada, I contacted a representative with Reno's district attorney's office to request a no contact order in addition to the assault charge. I also petitioned the courts to upgrade his charge to a felony due to the level of my injuries. Joe inflicted what was considered "sustainable bodily harm." I worked with the district attorney's office every step of the way to have the felony charges stick. Surely, I would receive justice with the courts in Reno for the horrific beating Joe inflicted on me.

Joe appeared before the judge in Reno three times. On his third appearance, he decided to take a plea bargain and entered a plea of no contest to a misdemeanor charge of domestic battery. For his crime, he received six months of online anger management courses and a fine of $300.00. If he stayed out of trouble for six months, then all charges would be downgraded to battery, which is a less severe crime than domestic battery.

I received a call from the victim's advocate in Reno late one afternoon. He told me the news, and I felt like I had been stabbed in the heart. *How could this be?* I thought to myself.

"I am sorry, Ms. Powers, but none of your paperwork was even reviewed by the district attorney's office. We have thousands of domestic violence cases each year and as far as the district attorney was concerned, you were out of state and out of mind," the victim's advocate explained.

He went on to tell me that I should be happy any charges were filed against Joe as most cases in Reno never even go before a judge.

"We have too many murders and severe cases to deal with here," he went on. "I am sorry, but it is over now."

"Thanks," I mumbled as I hung up. *For nothing,* I thought. Wow, and that was the victim's advocate who was supposed to be on my side.

I fought back tears as I headed to my rental car in the parking lot of my work. I could not believe it. I was nearly killed, and all Joe got was anger management classes and a small fine. How is that fair? How is that right? This is not justice but a mockery of the court system. I am sure Joe is laughing it up right about now. I climbed into my car and started the engine. At that moment, the Lord spoke directly to me as the words to the song on the radio blared, "It's not over yet."

I stopped dead in my tracks. *What?* I thought.

The Lord said to me, "Hope, do you not remember that I sit high above any authority on earth (Ephesians 1:21), including those judges in Reno? Believe me, when I say it's not over yet."

The Lord's voice was so crystal clear to me that day. I dried my eyes and drove home, rejoicing in my victory. I had no idea what the Lord meant by that, but I could not wait to see what He had planned.

A FEW WORDS ABOUT TOXIC PEOPLE AND RELATIONSHIPS

Another brief interuption of my story but I want to address the topic of toxic people and relationships as this has been a hard lesson for me to learn. We live in a fallen world, full of fallen people. I think we can all agree on that. We can encounter toxic people in all aspects of our life. Toxic people tend to lash out in anger when things do not go their way, either with words or violence. Some toxic people are more subtle through things like snide comments meant to hurt or tear down. Some withhold their affection or affirmation from others until they get their way. Many of us have even ended up in relationships that are toxic whether it be a work or personal relationship. We have all experienced this on one level or another.

We cannot fix toxic people!

Let me say that again, we cannot fix toxic people!

It is not our responsibility, it is God's. "Loving your neighbor" does not mean you enable them to abuse you in anyway. The Lord does not want us to be passive doormats nor does He want us to react in a sinful manner to the toxic person. Pray about the relationship with the toxic person, and then follow God's leading.

What does the Bible say about toxic people and relationships? Are we required to stay in these toxic relationships, especially with family members or your spouse? What if we cannot walk away? The Bible is full of warnings to Christians about associating with all types of toxic people. We should avoid these individuals at all cost in our walk with Christ. Some of the toxic people we should avoid include:

- those who betray you and spill innocent blood (Proverbs 16:29, Proverbs 1:10-12)

- those who are wicked and evil (Proverbs 4:14-17) Note the last part of this verse states that "Violence is their drug of choice." This is someone to avoid at all costs.

- those who gossip and are troublemakers (Proverbs 16:28)

- those who abuse others, participate in wild parties, drunkenness, and sexual promiscuity (1 Corinthians 6:9-10)

"Don't be naive. There are difficult times ahead. As the end approaches, people are going to be self-absorbed, money-hungry, self-promoting, stuck-up, profane, contemptuous of parents, crude, coarse, dog-eat-dog, unbending, slanderers, impulsively wild, savage, cynical, treacherous, ruthless, bloated windbags, addicted to lust, and allergic to God. They'll make a show of religion, but behind the scenes they're animals. Stay clear of these people."

2 TIMOTHY 3:1-5

The list could go on and on. I encourage you to do some research into this topic. There is so much information available in the Bible and other sources. I could write another book on this topic alone, but many are already available.

Most directly, we are told by the apostle Paul that we should not be in partnership with those who reject God (family members, spouses, and friends included). I can not emphasize this point enough!

"Don't become partners with those who reject God. How can you make a partnership out of right and wrong? That's not partnership; that's war. Is light best friends with dark? Does Christ go strolling with the Devil? Do trust and mistrust hold hands? Who would think of setting up pagan idols in God's holy Temple?"

2 CORINTHIANS 6:14-16
(SEE ALSO 1 CORINTHIANS 5:11-13, MATTHEW 18:20)

The Lord does not want us to be in abusive relationships whether it be with a parent, sibling, child, or spouse. If you are the one who is toxic, then confess your sins and repent. It is part of our sinful nature to be selfish and self-absorbed. We have all been there at least once in our lives, where we have said an unkind word in anger or been jealous over someone or something. This is part of being human. But if you cannot control your anger, bitterness, or other emotions that cause you to lash out repeatedly at someone that you love, seek professional help and maintain distance from the person who is the recipient.

Being physically abusive to anyone is a completely different ballgame. Understand that in the case of physical abuse, you have not only broken God's law but the laws of the land in which you live, and there are consequences, both now and eternally.

Physical abuse is completely unacceptible under any circumstance. Period.

> "So watch your step, friends. Make sure there's no evil unbelief lying around that will trip you up and throw you off course, diverting you from the living God."
>
> HEBREWS 3:12

My prayer to anyone reading these words who is suffering from any type of abuse, whether physical, mental, emotional, or spiritual, is that you would have the courage to say, "NO! NO MORE!" and walk away. I know the fear there is in doing this—fear of abandonment, fear of financial loss, fear of being isolated from your loved ones, and worst of all, fear of harm or death to you or your children (or others). I know this all too well. I lived it. I would encourage you to pray and SEEK HELP.

There are people, organizations, and agencies who will help you. I know from my experience that staying silent only gives the abuser more power over you. Not seeking help in this situation does not improve the circumstances. The abuser knows they can control you, and they thrive on this power. The more control you give them, the more power they have. The Lord does not want us to live in this type of bondage.

CHAPTER 6

LIVING THE HARSH REALITY

"How long do I have to put up with all this? How long till you haul my tormentors into court? The arrogant godless try to throw me off track, ignorant as they are of God and his ways. Everything you command is a sure thing, but they harass me with lies. Help!"
Psalm 119:84-86

THE DIVORCE

Following the hearing where the judge granted the order of protection against Joe, my attorney and I moved forward with the divorce proceedings. It was a long and tedious process. I was going to just give up and let Joe have everything, but my attorney persuaded me to think otherwise.

"How can you let this monster take all you have worked so hard to establish over the years, and on top of that he almost took your life?" my attorney asked convincingly.

"I just do not want to be put through this," I said. "I have already gone through so much. I do not want to prolong the proceedings and provoke his anger further."

My attorney assured me I would not be in danger as Joe knew to stay away from me due to the judge's admonishments. I knew Joe was broke, and his plan to kill me to collect my 401K and life insurance had failed. My attorney assured me that the law was on my side, and it might be a little struggle, but he saw a victory in the wings.

I reluctantly agreed to pursue what was rightfully mine from the courts and to seek restitution from Joe for my medical bills, which had mounted into the tens of thousands of dollars by this point. I also sought for my growing attorney's fees. I was feeling the financial impact hard, and it was difficult to maintain any sort of budget during this time as the medical bills and attorney fees often escalated without warning. I knew I could not continue this financial strain but told myself over and over it wasn't a choice right now. Somehow through God's amazing grace, I managed to survive financially.

My attorney and I, along with Joe and his attorney, appeared in court four or five times before the judge finally ordered us to go to mediation. I thought to myself, we will never settle this matter with a mediator, but God had already prepared the way.

During this difficult time of the civil proceedings, there appeared to be a glimmer of hope. Unbeknownst to me, one of the county's district attorneys and I would soon meet through God's providential arrangement to carry the criminal side of the case to another level once the divorce was settled.

GOING AFTER WHAT WAS LOST

(This part of the book was difficult to write as I sometimes feel consumed with fear but mostly anger. I know *all* things will be restored one day. "…every knee will bow, and every tongue confess…" Romans 14:11.)

The judge required Joe and I to go to mediation to split up the assets obtained in the marriage as Joe believed he was owed everything despite my financial contribution. There were my two precious dogs Joe bought for me, whom I loved dearly, paintings, pieces of jewelry, furniture, and the remainder of my personal effects. For months, I only had what I took to Reno along with a few things I was able to gather quickly following the assault. All my belongings were already sold at Joe's insistence, and I had to sell my car since Joe knew the make and model and often followed me. I drove a rental car for months before purchasing a vehicle. It seemed I had lost everything and had to start over.

I arrived at the mediator's office and a sheriff's deputy, who my attorney hired, met me in the parking lot. He explained that he was there for my safety and would remain with me until the mediation was over. The office of the mediator also hired an undercover police officer to protect their staff members because of Joe's history of violence both in actions and threats. Looking back on this, the shame is overwhelming at times. I wondered what was wrong with me that I did not see Joe for who he really was. What did I ever see in this violent, sadistic man? Why was I blind to his evil ways? Over and over, I praise God I was able to get away from him with my life, but the guilt and the shame of the whole incident remained.

I was taken into a meeting room at the mediator's office and asked to wait. I had all of God's promises written out on sticky notes in my hand and tried my best to keep calm. I felt like I could have a heart attack or

JOURNEY TO THE BEGINNING

faint at any moment. My attorney walked into the meeting room with the mediator. The mediator walked to the window and summoned my attorney and I to look outside as Joe had arrived and was standing next to his fancy sports car. He parked in a handicapped spot near the entry while smoking an electronic cigarette.

The mediator looked at me and asked, "Is he handicapped, Hope?"

"He thinks he deserves special treatment, but no I don't believe he is handicapped," I replied.

"What in the world were you thinking?" the mediator muttered as he walked back to the meeting room.

I only wish I knew and had an answer for him. This could not have been what God had in mind for me when I prayed all those months ago. I knew that once I had decided Joe was the one, I continued to pray but only briefly to thank God for sending Him to me and then moved on with the relationship. Had I forced what I thought was God's will? Should I have been more patient and not taken matters into my own hands? I thought I was stepping out in faith. Clearly now, this was not the case.

The negotiations went as one would expect. Joe would not agree to anything and demanded he keep everything. I had a list of everything I wanted from the relationship, but Joe would not relent to any of my requests. Joe and his attorney produced semi-nude pictures of me to the mediator. Joe had stolen these photographs from me sometime during our marriage and tried to use them to threaten me to give in to his demands. I had these boudoir photographs taken for my first husband years ago, but Joe claimed I was a stripper and prostitute and used these stolen photos as his evidence. The mediator was not swayed and commented to Joe that he was an idiot for not making the marriage work as I was quite beautiful. Joe burned with rage at this comment but was powerless to do anything.

Joe would not negotiate on the dogs he gave me, so I agreed that he could keep them. I had already obtained two new puppies for comfort and companionship for myself, as it had almost been a year since the assault and separation by this time. I was concerned that I had condemned those sweet little dogs to certain death by letting Joe have them, but I felt he would never let them go, and at least he treated them fairly well. I was not able to really care for four dogs as I would have liked to at this point, but I would have made a way to get those two precious dogs back.

Overall, I was able to negotiate to obtain the items I requested, barring the two puppies. This was primarily due to my attorney having the foresight to request a jury trial for the divorce. In other words, if we were not able to reach an agreement, the divorce would go to a jury trial instead of a judge's decision. While this would have cost more money, a jury trial would be a huge advantage for me. The mediator told Joe and his attorney that they wouldn't fare well in a jury trial as I looked like a sweet little girl who had been beaten and abused, whereas he resembled a frightening madman and even had the stereotypical look of a terrorist.

Joe took the mediator's advice and settled. I was happy we would not have to go to a jury trial because it would have been overwhelming for me. All that remained now was for Joe to sign the agreement and go before the judge again, so the divorce could be granted. Then, I would be free of that monster, at least legally.

PROVING UP

A court date was set on a Friday, a week or so after the mediation, to meet with the judge to review the progress in our divorce case. My attorney rushed to ensure that Joe had signed the papers before this date, so we could show the judge we had come to an agreement. Finally, the day prior to going before the judge, the papers were signed by all parties. My attorney informed me that this was just a brief hearing where the judge would set a time for Joe and me to return to the courts, so the divorce could be granted. The judge just wanted to confirm we followed his orders, in other words, "prove up" that we had done as he asked. My attorney told me that Joe and his attorney would not even be present.

I prayed long and hard over this hearing as I knew something amazing was going to happen. The Lord spoke to me and told me that not only would we "prove up" on this day to the judge, who ordered the mediation, but that this judge would send us to the family courts, and the divorce would be granted. When we arrived at the courthouse, I told my attorney what was going to happen that day with the judge and that it would finally be over. He cautioned me not to get my hopes up as this scenario was unlikely, and he had never seen this judge do anything like that before, especially on a Friday. As we entered the courtroom, I told my attorney to stand back and watch the Lord work and be amazed!

After what seemed like an eternity, the bailiff finally called our case. Praise God, Joe and his attorney were a no show. I approached the bench with confidence but still felt a bit stressed. My attorney handed all the signed paperwork to the judge. The judge reviewed them then asked why Joe and his attorney were not in attendance.

My attorney shook his head and shrugged his shoulders and said, "I cannot say your honor."

The judge looked at me and asked me if I was ready for this to be over.

I answered, "Yes, your honor."

"Then it will be over today," the judge exclaimed. "Go to the family court judge, and she will finish with the proceedings to grant the divorce." The judge looked at me and smiled.

As my attorney and I exited the courtroom, he looked at me with a shocked and puzzled look.

"How did you know this would happen?" he asked.

"I trusted God," I told my attorney.

He, also a Christian, stood in amazement just as I knew he would. I jokingly asked him if he did not remember that God set Jesus in high authority over all the rulers of earth?

"Yes, of course," he laughed, "but in my experience in this court, it did not seem likely to happen. I guess I should have had faith in God's words."

We exchanged smiles and headed down the hall to the family court.

"...God raised him from death and set him on a throne in deep heaven, in charge of running the universe, everything from galaxies to governments, no name and no power exempt from his rule."

EPHESIANS 1:20-21

When we entered in the family court room, there was no one waiting, and it appeared that the judge was finishing another case. The bailiff took the paperwork from my attorney and told us to have a seat as it would only be a few minutes. My attorney and I sat down but were almost immediately called to go before the judge. The judge asked me three or four questions, and then it was over. She granted the divorce and said I could pick up a copy of the paperwork in about ten days from the registrar's office. My attorney told me to go home and relax for the weekend. It was finally over, and I was free from that monster! Praise God!

When Joe heard that the divorce had been granted without his presence, he was furious, but he could not do anything. It was over! Now, all that remained was for Joe to bring all my belongings to a neutral location, so I could pick them up. He had twenty days to do this.

LIVING IN A NIGHTMARE

During the months leading up to the mediation and then divorce, I battled a demonic presence that seemed to have followed me from Joe. Night after night, I suffered severe torture and physical abuse that left visible bruises on my body from the demonic presence that followed me, not to mention the horrific nightmares that ensued. I prayed desperately for relief from these attacks but could not seem to shake myself of these evil spirits. I tried to rid myself of anything that might be a conduit of evil in my possession, but it did not seem to offer relief. I share my experiences as an example of God's deliverance from evil during this terrible point in my life.

One night as I lay in bed tossing and turning, I could not keep evil thoughts about Joe out of my head. I wished something terrible would happen to him or that he would die, and I would never have to ever deal with him again. The Lord reprimanded me for this often and told me I had no idea how He could use someone like Joe. I was reminded of Saul's conversion on the road to Damascus and Jesus casting out seven demons from Mary Magdalene. Then the scripture would pop into my mind like, "I'm in charge of vengeance and payback, just waiting for them to slip up; and the day of their doom is just around the corner, sudden and swift and sure." (Deuteronomy 32:35).

I would repent of this sin repeatedly, but for some reason, on this night, I could not seem to shake this awful feeling. This went on for hours as I tossed and turned, wrestling with these terrible feelings. Finally, I decided it was time to call in the big guns. I cried to the Lord to send Michael, His archangel, to my rescue to fight these enemies. As I prayed and cried out to God for his help, I could feel the air change in the room. It is hard to describe this feeling except to say the air was stirring. Maybe a minute or two after I cried out, a calmness started to overtake me, and I began to relax. I thanked God that He rescued me from these evil thoughts. About that time, the smoke alarm went off in my room. It did not go off in Joshua's room or in any other room in the apartment. The alarm did not sound anywhere else in the apartment complex. It was limited to my room only. Joshua did not even hear it.

I imagined that Michael's flaming sword had set off the smoke alarm. I looked up as the alarm stopped going off and immediately felt, not heard, an inaudible voice say, "Oops, sorry about that." Maybe it was my imagination, but I believe God sent Michael to fight off the evil forces that were attacking me that night. I believe the smoke alarm went off that night, so I would know God sent His angels to fight on my behalf. I praised God for all the times He has rescued me, again and again. I closed my eyes and drifted peacefully off to sleep.

"For he will command his angels concerning you
to guard you in all your ways."

PSALM 91:11 NIV

THE CLOSET

Another lonely night, several months following the assault and separation and a few weeks from the last incident, I could not sleep per usual. I tossed and turned relentlessly. There was something there, and I felt its presence. I prayed diligently to be delivered from this evil. During my fervent prayers, I was drawn to my closet. There was something in the closet I must confront. I was terrified beyond belief but more afraid to leave it be.

As I entered the closet, I was drawn to a stack of books. I had already been through these books several times and discarded the ones possibly related to the occult or entry points for evil to move into my home. I frantically started searching the books again. There was nothing there but my devotional and exercise books. I could not find anything, yet I continued to be drawn to them. I knew there was something there I was missing. I decided to pull each of the books out and thumb through them to see if there was something inside one of the books I had forgotten.

About halfway through this process, I saw it. There was a book that had fallen behind the others and was completely hidden behind the shelf. I reached to grab the book to pull it out and as I touched it, the temperature in the closet dropped about thirty degrees. A terrifying chill overtook me as I pulled the book out of its hiding place and saw the cover. I had purchased the book when I was in New Orleans on business as a gift for Joe. It described the haunted houses and cemeteries throughout New Orleans and described how Voodoo and other non-Christian religions influenced the growing occult in the area. The author had signed it, so it indeed had the handiwork of the devil attached to it.

At this point, I panicked. I cried out to God to spare me from this evil. All I knew is that I had to get this book out of my home as soon as possible, but how? By this time, it was late, and I did not want to walk out in the dark alone. No telling what would be waiting for me there. God formulated a plan for me. I ran into the kitchen, gathered up the trash, ran to the closet, and put the book inside. I tied the trash bag in triple knots and placed another bag around it to ensure the evil did not escape. If I could only get the trash to the dumpster, it would be incinerated. But the dumpster was an exceptionally long way from my apartment, and it was late and very dark.

Not sure what I should do at this point, I put the trash bag outside of the front door and went back into my room to contemplate my options. As I reentered the bedroom closet to turn the light off, immediately, the temperature returned to normal. I knew Joshua would be home soon, so I texted him to ask him to take the trash to the dumpster when he arrived. I told him not to ask questions but to take the trash bag immediately to the dumpster before he entered the apartment. It was critical that he do this for me.

By this point, Joshua was used to my strange requests, so he did not question anything and replied that he would take the bag to the dumpster before entering the apartment. He told me he would be home soon and that I should not worry, he would take care of it. I trusted he would follow through with my wishes, so I lay back in my bed and drifted peacefully off to sleep.

The next morning, I awoke to Joshua sleeping peacefully in his room and then went and opened the front door to ensure the trash bag was gone. Indeed, it was. My son had taken it to the dumpster as I had requested. As the morning wore on, Joshua finally awoke, and we sat to eat breakfast and talked about the events of the week. As we were discussing our week, I was reminded of the trash bag last night. I promptly thanked him for taking this to the dumpster and him not questioning me on this.

He looked at me as if I had two heads and said, "Mom, you must really be losing it. There was no trash bag outside the front door when I got home."

At that moment, I felt a chill run down my spine. What happened to the bag? Did someone else pick it up that late at night? I lived on the third floor in a corner so there was no way someone could have accidently walked by and took it. It was too late for the nightly trash pick up to run, plus they had already come for the night, and I had gathered my trash can back inside the apartment.

I will never know what happened to that trash bag, but I do know this, God's hand was covering me that night. The bag was removed by good not evil forces to ensure my safety and that of my son's. This was another great miracle of how God showed me that HE was working in my life. The cliché of "taking out the trash" has a new meaning for me. Perhaps this was God showing me that I could purge my life of evil. No more garbage.

"Compared to the high privilege of knowing Christ Jesus as my Master, firsthand, everything I once thought I had going for me is insignificant—dog dung. I've dumped it all in the trash so that I could embrace Christ and be embraced by him."

PHILIPPIANS 3:8

THE PURGING

"Summing it all up, friends, I'd say you'll do best by filling
your minds and meditating on things true, noble, reputable,
authentic, compelling, gracious—the best, not the worst; the
beautiful, not the ugly; things to praise, not things to curse."

PHILIPPIANS 4:8

Day after day, I did everything I knew to purge any evil attached to my
life. I asked for prayer from the saints in my life, and they always would
tell me I should focus on what is right, noble, pure, and praiseworthy,
not the demonic. I tried over and over to do this, but I finally could not
take it anymore, and I showed a friend some pictures of the bruises I was
acquiring daily. Finally, she agreed to introduce me to someone who she
thought might be able to help me.

There was a man, a missionary, who went to our church and had worked
in countries where there had been demon possessions, and she thought
that maybe he could help me. The next Sunday, she introduced me to
him and told him a little bit about my story. Following the service, he
asked if I was ready to be rid of these demons. Of course, I was—I was
more than ready. He explained to me that things could happen to me
if I truly was demon possessed and that I might get sick or faint as the
demons left me. I did not care. I just wanted to be free, so I agreed to do
whatever he asked me to do.

He had me pray with him, and I prayed that prayer more passionately
than anyone had ever prayed it according to his wife. Nothing happened
to me. I was not demon possessed, but he agreed that for some reason
I was being attacked by demons in my home. He could not say exactly

what the cause was but that he could get rid of them. I told him about my encounters with Joe, and he said this was likely the cause, but he could not rule out that the apartment where I currently lived could have had someone who lived there prior to me that practiced witchcraft or something related to the occult. We planned a time that he would come to my home to anoint the doorways and windows. He agreed to let me know if he felt any evil presence in my home, and we would pray against that evil and drive it out. I was so thrilled that I might finally get relief.

The day finally arrived that he and his wife were going to come to my apartment. I invited the friend I had confided in as well, so there were four of us. I told Joshua I was having people from my church come over, and it was probably not a good idea that he be there. He agreed as he had plans anyway, so after he greeted everyone, he left. The missionary walked throughout my home and prayed. His wife, my friend, and I stayed in the living room and prayed while he walked through every room of the house. I heard him pray the blood of Jesus as he anointed the windows and the doorways with oil.

When he finished his prayers and anointing of the windows and doorways, he asked me to come into my bedroom. He said he found one thing where he felt a demonic presence. He would not tell me what it was but asked me to enter my room and to see if I could feel it as well. I did not have to feel it because I could see it. I saw a demon as plain as day in the painting hanging above the headboard, and I expressed my concern to him. He then told me that he could not see the demon, but this was the very object that he felt had a demonic presence. We left my bedroom, and he told me that it was up to me as to what I should do with that painting. All he intended to do was to identify if there were any objects or areas where there was a demonic presence in my apartment. I thanked him and his wife, as well as my friend, for coming over to help purge my life of this demonic presence.

As they were leaving, the missionary turned to me and said, "Hope, do you not know that you have the power to call out demons in Jesus's name?"

I replied, "I guess, but I just didn't think that I was capable of doing this."

He said, "Yes, Jesus has given you and I the authority."

I knew in my heart that I would never have to be afraid of this evil again. After everyone left, I was alone in the apartment with the demon in the painting. What was I going to do? How was I going to get rid of this painting? I could not leave it hanging, especially over my head! I must be brave and get rid of it, I thought to myself. I walked in and pulled that painting right off the wall. As I was removing the painting, I noticed the back label. It reminded me of where and when I purchased it. I was immediately taken aback with the fact that this demon was not related to Joe, but it was my own demon from years before meeting him.

I had purchased the painting years before I met Joe, and the circumstances surrounding the time and location of the purchase was of great remorse for me. My sinful nature had overtaken my better judgement during this time in my life, and I had never truly forgiven myself. The Lord showed me at that moment that it was my own unforgiveness causing my pain. I felt as if the weight of the world had been lifted off my shoulders. I do believe that the demons that persecuted me originally came from Joe, but after all my purging and prayers of deliverance, the one that remained was brought in by me. Once I removed the painting, the tormenting stopped.

ONE FINAL ATTEMPT

Following the missionary's visit, one final attempt was made by a demon to enter my home. I was having dinner after a long day at work, and

I looked out the window and saw a demon floating in mid-air with its eyes glowing red. I was terrified. When I saw it, it briefly looked at me, and then my tiny four-pound dog went into spasms and convulsions.

"Oh, no!" I screamed. "You are not taking my dog. In the name of Jesus Christ, get out of here."

At that moment, my sweet little dog passed out on the ground and stopped shaking. I scooped her up and her little heart was beating so fast as was mine.

"It's okay," I comforted her, "nothing will harm us."

My dog recovered quickly and had no lasting effects from the demon's attack. Following this incident, no demons ever tried to enter my home again. Praise God!

THE TOLL OF EVIL

The trials and demonic attacks wreaked havoc on me. I was constantly in fight or flight mode. I could barely eat anything during this time and lost about fifty pounds. My weight dropped dangerously low when I hit rock bottom, and I could barely function. I tried to eat but could not. I knew I could not continue like this, but it seemed like the trials and tribulations would never end.

My weight loss did not go unnoticed. Some people at work started to gossip about me. "Maybe she has cancer," some would say. "She is definitely sick," others would say. All in all, it was a very difficult time. I knew I must depend on the Lord, and He would see me through as He is faithful, but it was a long and difficult struggle. I took comfort in Paul's description of his imprisonment and difficult times in Asia, knowing that despite the difficult times, I could trust in God's strength, not my own.

"We don't want you in the dark, friends, about how hard it was when all this came down on us in Asia province. It was so bad we didn't think we were going to make it. We felt like we'd been sent to death row, that it was all over for us. As it turned out, it was the best thing that could have happened. Instead of trusting in our own strength or wits to get out of it, we were forced to trust God totally—not a bad idea since he's the God who raises the dead! And he did it, rescued us from certain doom. And he'll do it again, rescuing us as many times as we need rescuing."

2 CORINTHIANS 1:8-10

After the divorce was final, I worked hard to regain my life. I wanted to get back to my routines and things I enjoyed again after an absence of more than eighteen months. I gained about twenty pounds back, so I was in a much better place health-wise, even though I still needed to gain another ten pounds or so to be at a healthy weight.

"You realize, don't you, that you are the temple of God, and God himself is present in you? No one will get by with vandalizing God's temple, you can be sure of that. God's temple is sacred—and you, remember, are the temple."

1 CORINTHIANS 3:16-17

At that time, I did not realize that I was going to need to be healthy for the next battle I would be required to fight, not in my own strength but in God's strength.

GOD'S INTERVENTION—GOD SEES US!

Back when I was battling the divorce and ongoing demonic assaults, I was not sitting still. I wanted to get involved in advocacy for those coming out of domestic violence, as this helped channel the nervous energy I had. I felt that in a way, I could be helping do God's handiwork. I inquired about a local women's shelter in my neighborhood, and before long, I was able to speak with the director, who invited me to visit the office. I did not know this center even existed, or I would have reached out to them in my crisis.

I was thrilled to take a day to visit. I was able to talk to the women who worked at the center and tell them what happened to me. I watched videos of testimonies from abused women, toured apartments designed for abused women, who were just getting back on their feet, and got to tour the safe house at an undisclosed location where women could hide from their abusers. I was impressed, not only with the facilities, but with the women working there. I was not quite ready to volunteer just yet, but they were not at all disappointed and encouraged me to take some more time.

One of the ladies I met that day invited me to lunch the next week, so I agreed to go. This started a friendship I would soon value greatly. We had lunch about once a month and stayed connected through emails. After more than six months of correspondence, she asked if I might be interested in speaking about my situation. It was October, which is domestic violence awareness month, so her organization was inundated with requests for speakers. I told her I would love to, although I was

LIVING THE HARSH REALITY

very nervous. She could not tell me right away which location I would speak at, but she would make the arrangements, and we would travel to the location together. She explained that this was a very special request. I was a little intimidated, but I felt God leading me to do this.

About a week before this event, my new friend told me I would be speaking to the county's district attorney's office. She explained that the entire office was completing training in domestic violence awareness, and they wanted someone to speak about their circumstances. She said they chose me because I had not used any of the services provided by the center, so I could be completely unbiased. I was stunned and frightened. Could I speak without breaking down? Would my nerves get the best of me, and I just run out? I prayed, and the Lord told me, "Do not be afraid, I am with you. I will tell you what to say."

I was told I would speak for thirty minutes and then allow ten to fifteen minutes of questions. Overall, I was scheduled for an hour but did not have to use all of it. But regardless, thirty minutes was a long time to speak. Would I have enough to say for thirty minutes of time? What if the audience did not like me? So many negative thoughts ran through my mind, but God was right there countering them all.

THE BIG DAY

The day arrived, and I was nervous. My friend told me to come early to the center and practice for some of the ladies. They were there to support me, and I could certainly use the practice. I arrived at the women's center at the designated time and practiced my speech in front of my avid supporters. As I was speaking, the women began to cry. I was shocked. By the time I finished, there was not a dry eye in the room. *Oh no*, I thought to myself, *hopefully it was not that bad.*

My friend who worked at the center told me it was an amazing story, and she was moved greatly. The other ladies concurred and commented on how I was going to shake up the district attorney's office.

"It's not me," I said. "It is the Lord speaking through me."

Following the practice session, we all went to lunch, but I was too nervous to eat. The time flew by, and soon it was time to head to the courthouse for my speech. I invited a church friend to come hear my story. She was a big support for me during the stalking and order of protection trial. When I walked in, she was waiting for me at the door, and I greeted her with a big hug. I was so thankful she was there.

We went into the building where I was greeted by the training coordinator, who was a beautiful young woman, who started at the district attorney's office right out of college. She was kind and gentle in nature, and her manner was reassuring to me.

"Here is some water in case you get a dry throat during your speech," she said. "Everyone here is so excited to hear your story. Thank you for sharing this with us."

She led me into a room, a very large room. I was not sure what I expected, but I had no idea this many people worked at the district attorney's office. She explained that there would be eighty or ninety police officers, probation officers, and others in attendance.

"I can do all things through Christ who gives me strength," I silently told myself as she led me to my seat.

"You will kick off the next session that starts in about ten minutes," she said. "Do you need anything?"

"No," I said. "Thank you."

"Ok then, when it's time, I will introduce you to the group," she said as she walked away.

The participants started to trickle into the room. I began to panic, but I prayed, and a calmness came over me. The time came, and the young woman introduced me to the crowd. I walked to the microphone and introduced myself and told a little about my background. I explained to them that I told these things not to brag or boast but to show that domestic violence was an equal opportunity predator and that no group of age, ethnicity, education, gender, social status, or religion was beyond its reach. I then went on to tell them I was going to read from a transcript I had written as I did not want to forget to say anything important or leave anything out. Every eye was watching as they sat in silence, waiting for me to tell my story.

Here are the last few lines:

> *In conclusion, I believe that where there was once paralyzing fear, there will be eternal hope; where there was once unimaginable evil, there will be unfathomable good; where there was once contempt and disdain, there will be respect and honor; where there was once immeasurable loss and sadness, there will be endless joy and restoration.*

I chose to end the speech by summarizing the lyrics from the song "Live it Well" by Switchfoot, as this seemed to best describe how I was feeling at the time and my need for confession of my sin and drawing closer to God through this situation. I love the reason that the songwriters wrote these words, as they explained, "With confession comes freedom. Freedom to be authentic. Freedom to embrace the life you have been given. Freedom to live a life of meaning and purpose, even against the backdrop of pain and disappointment, because the One who breathed you into existence loves you. Because the kingdom of the heaven is at hand." [4]

This is where I am, right here, right now, I thought and smiled as I finished the speech.

As I concluded, I looked up at the audience. Numerous people were weeping, and others were blotting their eyes. Even some of the men were crying. I was shocked as a roar of applause erupted from the audience, and then people started standing and clapping. What? WOW! *The Lord got a standing ovation,* I thought, as I could barely remember speaking. My hostess came to the podium with tears in her eyes and told me how moving this speech was. She looked at the audience and asked if there were any questions. Immediately about a dozen hands went up. They probably had the same questions you have. Why did you not leave? Why did you marry him? Why did you not call the police?

The questions went on and on, and my hostess intervened, "Please, our guest has been through a traumatic event, do not overwhelm her."

"It is fine," I said, "I want to answer the questions."

I tried my best to explain my mindset and terror during this time. Over and over in my speech, I inserted the phrase, "I was terrified for my life and for the life of my children."

The hostess came back to the podium, even though there were more questions, and told the group, "We have gone over our time and must get back on our schedule."

Where had the time gone? I thought. It seemed like minutes, not two hours.

"Hope, we have a gift for you," said my hostess. "We are bestowing the county's medal of honor on you for your bravery for surviving this horrific ordeal and having the courage to tell us your story."

"Thank you, I don't know what to say," I said. But my words were drowned out with another round of applause. Thank you, Lord, for your faithfulness, I murmured as I walked away from the podium.

The ladies from the women's center, my friend from church, and I walked out of the district attorney's office. I could not believe I had just spoken to this large group without faltering. They commented how proud they were of me, but I know it was the Lord who was speaking that day. He had plans for me. I gave my church friend a hug and headed to my car. Yes indeed, the Lord had plans I could have never envisioned.

"God is striding ahead of you. He's right there with you. He won't let you down; he won't leave you. Don't be intimidated. Don't worry."

DEUTERONOMY 31:8

THE CALL THAT CHANGED MY LIFE

I survived the speech I delivered (or should I say the Lord delivered) to the district attorney's office, so now it was time to relax and enjoy my trip to the National Coalition Against Domestic Violence Conference. The conference was slated for four days just outside of Phoenix, Arizona, so I took a week of vacation to have extra days for sightseeing. I left Joshua in charge of the dogs, so I felt that I could finally get away a bit to relax.

It was an amazing time of reflection and learning more about others who shared similar experiences. I was shocked at the stories, and although I was not ready at that time to tell my story to an audience of this size, I benefited greatly from hearing from others. There were family members who told horror stories of their loved ones being killed in a domestic situation and even a mother who had lost three young daughters to an enraged spouse who had kidnapped and then killed them. It was gut wrenching to hear these stories, but there was always a message of hope and healing.

On the third day of the conference, I received a voice message. It was one of the district attorneys named Tom Gordon, who attended the session on the Friday before. His message was simple enough, "Hello, Ms. Powers, this is Tom Gordon from the district attorney's office. I attended the session where you shared your story, and I would like for you to give me a callback."

When I received the message, I thought it was a bit odd that he had gotten my number but figured he probably had access to this through the women's center. Later that day, I returned his call and was amazed at what he had to say.

"Hello, thank you for returning my call, Ms. Powers. Everyone at the district attorney's office was so moved by your story. I personally have not been able to sleep since hearing this, and we have all decided to see if there is anything we can do to help put this madman behind bars. If there is one thing he did to you while in our area, we want to pursue this. Would you be willing to come and talk to us, and let us see if there might be something we can charge him with?"

I was shocked and did not know what to say. "Sure, I am happy to come and talk to you further," I said.

"When can you come?" Mr. Gordon asked.

I explained that I was at the conference and would be home on Friday morning. He asked if I could come on that Friday afternoon.

"Sure," I said, "I will see you then." I could not believe the turn of events. *When the Lord decides to move, He is not slow,* I thought to myself.

THE QUESTIONING

After returning from the conference, I headed back to the district attorney's office. I went through the metal detector and went up the elevator to the district attorney's floor. I entered the reception area and told my name to the woman behind the bulletproof glass.

"Yes, Ms. Powers," she said, "Mr. Gordon will be out soon."

I took a seat as police officers and others came in and exited on the elevator. Soon enough, Mr. Gordon came out and introduced himself to me.

"Thank you for coming, Ms. Powers," he said, "We are all anxious to talk with you. Please follow me."

I followed Mr. Gordon into a large conference room down the hall from where I spoke the week prior, and there were several people there waiting for me. Mr. Gordon introduced them to me. There was another district attorney, a victim's advocate, and a police officer present. I was a bit intimidated, but Mr. Gordon soon put me at ease by saying that they just wanted to ask me a few questions. He explained that all these people were present to comply with the law should they decide to pursue a case against Joe. He went on to explain that based on my answers to their questions, they could decide whether they have a case, and if not, they would not have me continue as they did not want to cause me any further distress. Mr. Gordon told me that I was free to stop answering any of their questions at any time, and if it became too painful for me to continue, they would not pursue anything further with me.

"I understand," I said.

"Let's get started," Mr. Gordon said.

I agreed, and he started to question me regarding my experiences with Joe. After three questions, Mr. Gordon stopped the questioning and asked the other district attorney if she could join him in the hallway for one moment. I immediately thought to myself that this was not a good sign. There must not be enough evidence from my answering those few questions to charge Joe. I had tried, but I guess it was not enough or either too much time had gone by. I waited for their return so they could give me the news.

After about ten minutes, the door opened, and there were several people who I had not seen before who entered the meeting room. Mr. Gordon introduced them to me, and then explained that in the few questions I had answered, it was apparent there were numerous violations of the law that came with prison time, and some were serious felonies Joe had committed. The district attorney's office wished to pursue these charges against Joe but wanted to make sure they did everything according to the law so there were no loopholes on procedural issues Joe could claim in his defense. *This was really happening,* I thought to myself. I think I knew what God meant when He told me, "It's not over yet," on the day that the Reno court had given Joe a slap on the wrist for almost killing me.

Once they set up the video camera and started to record my statement, I retold every detail as best as I could remember. I even demonstrated the arm holds that Joe would put on me on Mr. Gordon.

"Wow, that really hurts," he commented.

"Sorry," I said.

The district attorney asked questions, and they recorded my answers for hours, late into the evening. Finally, as we wrapped up for the night,

Mr. Gordon told me, "Thank you, Ms. Powers. Maybe I can sleep now knowing that we can get this guy."

I smiled and said, "I hope so, as he is already after other women by now even though our divorce is not yet final."

"Don't worry," Mr. Gordon said, "enjoy your weekend knowing that you have taken steps to bring a criminal to justice."

I smiled, and a police officer showed up to escort me to my car. The officer took me out a back entrance and told me that this was protocol for witnesses where domestic violence was implicated. I thanked him and drove home. I could not wait to tell Joshua all about my trip and the day at the district attorney's office. He would not believe it, as I could barely believe it.

THE GRAND JURY

Although the district attorney continued to investigate all my claims, spoke to witnesses, and got his case together, he wanted the divorce to be finalized before proceeding with the grand jury hearing so that Joe would not use this as leverage in the divorce proceedings. Somehow Joe found out and started to make threats through his attorney that I better drop any charges against him, or he would not sign the divorce decree. At this point, my divorce attorney told Joe's attorney that it was in the hands of the state now, and I could not stop the proceedings even if I wanted to. Joe's attorney threated numerous times to sue me for slander and defamation of character, but as my attorney pointed out to him, it was only slander and defamation of character if I said things that were not true. This kept Joe's attorney quiet for a while. My attorney then stopped replying to the demands of Joe's attorney, and Joe eventually went to the mediation and signed the paperwork to complete the divorce (as I previously described).

Several months after the divorce was final, I received a call from the district attorney that he would be taking the charges to the grand jury. He explained that there would be three felony charges filed against Joe. There were two charges of assault with a deadly weapon, one charge each with a gun and a knife, respectively, and one charge of aggravated stalking, which also was considered a felony. Both assault charges carried a sentence of twenty years in jail, and the aggravated stalking charge carried a sentence of ten years in jail. If Joe were convicted of all charges, he could potentially, in a perfect world, face up to fifty years in prison.

However, the first step was to get a conviction by the grand jury. This would determine if there was enough evidence to even pursue a conviction for any or all these crimes against Joe. The district attorney told me it could go either way. If we did not get a conviction from the grand jury, then it was over. We would have to wait and see how it goes. There were no witnesses in the grand jury hearing, so I had to patiently wait for the outcome. I prayed to God that His justice would prevail.

> "Don't hit back; discover beauty in everyone. If you've got it in you, get along with everybody. Don't insist on getting even; that's not for you to do. "I'll do the judging," says God. "I'll take care of it."
>
> ROMANS 12:17-19

I sat anxiously by the phone, for what seemed like hours. Finally, the phone rang. It was Mr. Gordon.

"We got a conviction on all three counts from the grand jury. The police have issued a warrant for Joe's arrest. He will be picked up and jailed shortly," he explained. "You will receive a call when he is arrested so stay by your phone."

I could not believe it. I thanked God for this decision and prayed Joe would not threaten harm to me or my family ever again.

Shortly, I received a call from an anonymous number. "Ms. Powers, this is Carl Jones, federal marshal. We are trying to pick up Joe and we wanted your help in locating him," said the voice on the other end of the line.

"I am not sure where he would have gone, unless he went to see his daughter," I stated.

Mr. Jones said, "No problem, we will wait him out and call you back."

"Thank you, sir," I said. "I am concerned that he may try to put up a fight with you. He has threatened to never surrender to police."

"Thank you for your concern for our safety, Ms. Powers, but we can manage this situation. I am a profiler, and although he threatened this, he is not one to act on it." Officer Jones continued, "We will be in touch."

I felt relieved that the officers knew what they were getting into, but I still prayed for their safety.

Several hours passed and I received a call back from Mr. Jones. "We got him," he stated.

"Did he put up a fight or make threats?" I questioned.

"No, he went without incident," Mr. Jones explained. "He was with his girlfriend, and he gave her the keys to his apartment and told her to take the dogs, and then he came right along with us."

"Do you think his girlfriend will come after me?" I asked.

He said, "Ms. Powers, let me have a little talk with you, dear, as this man is still controlling you, and it needs to stop."

He was quite sincere in his explanation.

"I have been doing this job for thirty years now, and I have been a profiler for the federal marshal's office for more than two decades," he continued, "and I have never seen a situation where someone like this can persuade others to do his bidding or that he will seek revenge on you. This man is a psychopath, meaning he is incapable of any type of feelings, and he has long forgotten you and moved on to his next victim. Why would he continue to pursue you when there are so many others out there that he can manipulate?"

I saw his point, and it helped alleviate my fears somewhat, but I remembered all the threats Joe made.

"Like the threats of death by cop," Mr. Jones commented and laughed. "Nothing more than words but take precautions," Mr. Jones continued, "and in the event I am wrong, which I never am, here is my personal cell phone number. Call this number at any time that you see Joe, or he threatens you again. I promise you; we will have someone right there. We have agents close by."

I thanked him for his help, and I did feel better. He was right, so far, as I have never had to use that number.

Joe was in jail for six days, much longer than expected by the district attorney. The judge would not release Joe until he had an ankle monitor hooked up, so he could be tracked. This took days to complete, plus Joe had to pay the bail. I was still in awe at how God was working all things out.

CHAPTER 7
THE END OR JUST THE BEGINNING?

"I have it all planned out—plans to take care of you, not abandon you, plans to give you the future you hope for."
Jeremiah 29:11

I felt free, but I knew this freedom would not be long lived as Joe would eventually get out of jail and the threats may once again escalate. What would I do, what could I do? I took comfort in knowing he was outfitted with an ankle monitor and that if he were to come near to where I lived or worked, I would be alerted. I did not trust that system, so I stayed vigilant and strong, but it was difficult to do. I had come this far, and there was no turning back. It was out of my hands and now in the hands of the state. I knew it was in God's hands, and He sits in much higher authority than all the rulers in the world. No one is exempt from His rule. It gave me great peace to know that Jesus has the final word.

"All this energy issues from Christ: God raised him from death and set him on a throne in deep heaven, in charge of running the universe, everything from galaxies to governments, no name and no power exempt from his rule. And not just for the time being, but forever. He is in charge of it all, has the final word on everything."

EPHESIANS 1:20-22

WHAT IF THE END IS JUST THE BEGINNING?

I knew the next months would be difficult, so I tried not to think about it, yet it seemed to consume my every thought. Mr. Gordon wanted to be ready for trial quickly to catch Joe's attorney off guard. I had compiled a list of names for Mr. Gordon to contact to corroborate my story. I had hundreds, if not thousands, of text messages, voicemails, emails, and other incriminating evidence against Joe. Mr. Gordon had a forensic expert remove all the text messages, voicemails, and emails from my phone and computer. I also had stacks of medical bills by this time, including bills from seeing a Christian counselor. I tried to regain some normalcy in my life, but the trial was looming over my head.

While three indictments had been handed down by the grand jury, Mr. Gordon decided to pursue the strongest case of aggravated stalking. The aggravated stalking charge was a felony crime that carried a sentence of ten years maximum. Mr. Gordon explained to me that if we could get a conviction of the maximum sentence, then it might be worth pursuing the other two charges of aggravated assault with a deadly weapon. Given the current court system in the United States, this was an unlikely scenario, but one worth using as leverage. Regardless of the outcome, Joe had three felony charges hanging over his head. He had been indicted for each and would soon be out of jail with an ankle monitor.

FALSE ACCUSATIONS, LIES, AND OTHER UNTRUTHS

His attorney, who was the same one from the divorce and was inapt at criminal law (praise God), submitted all kinds of evidence against me to try to intimidate the district attorney to drop the case. Joe claimed he had evidence that I was a prostitute and a stripper. This was ludicrous and absurd, but Joe had stolen my old phones and computers and conveniently removed bits and pieces of conversations along with photos from when I was married to my ex-husband.

After my first divorce, I dated other men. Some of them were serious relationships, but they all failed. Joe used this to his advantage to try and embarrass me. This was a dark time for me, and even though I prayed and sought Jesus night and day, it was hard to get a reprieve from the near daily accusations. I dreaded seeing the phone ring with the caller ID for the district attorney's office. I was afraid he would give up on me and drop the case due to the false accusations. I knew I had made mistakes in my life, but was I not redeemable?

The abusive words from my first husband and Joe constantly rang in my head over and over. "You are nothing! No one would want you. You are old and ugly. The only thing you will have to look forward to is death."

This barrage of insults and accusations lasted for months. It seemed as if I would never be free. However, Mr. Gordon was persistent and contacted all my leads to counter the claims that Joe and his attorney made against me. He even contacted my ex-husband. At least Mr. Gordon believed me.

CAN I EVER HAVE A NORMAL LIFE?

Meanwhile, eighteen months into this madness, I had met a man named Bob. This was about two months prior to Joe's arrest. Bob was kind and gentle. He lived in the same building I did and saw me when I came in to sign the lease. He said that he was immediately attracted to me and made a point of introducing himself as a welcome to the building. At the time, I never thought twice about it, except to think that the people here were nice. I saw Bob several times in the hallway or parking garage. He always spoke and asked me how I was doing. He was kind and often volunteered to help me if there was anything I needed. I politely nodded, but these thoughts escaped my mind as soon as I walked away.

Bob was persistent in his pursuit, and one day as I was walking my dogs, he was there on the path. "Hello there," he said. "I did not know you had dogs."

"Yes," I replied, "two little crazy dogs."

Bob then asked me if I had any big plans for the weekend. Of course, I was again naïve to his intentions and replied that I was looking forward to a little R & R and of course, church on Sunday.

"Good," Bob replied. "Then you are free to join me tonight for dinner."

Wait, what? I thought. Did he just sneak that in without my knowledge? I guess the look on my face showed I was about to politely decline.

Bob said, "Oh come on, what could it hurt? It is only dinner, and I can meet you there. You pick the place. I will not take no for an answer. You look like you could use a nice dinner."

"Well, I guess I could meet you somewhere," I hesitantly said. We lived in walking distance of several upscale restaurants, so he told me to pick the place. I explained that I had never been to any of these places, so whichever one he decided on was fine. We agreed on a time and place.

As Bob departed, he turned and said, "See you soon, Hope."

It dawned on me that I did not even remember his name.

The dinner went well, and it was nice to have company for a change. Thank God Bob mentioned his name, so I did not have to admit I could not remember it. I made it clear that I was a Christian and had a high moral standard. He was agreeable to this and shared the same morals and values. After dinner, I walked back home. Bob lived on the same floor as I did, but I told him I was fine to walk to my apartment alone. He was respectful of this and told me to text him when I arrived at my apartment. I followed his request and texted that I had much appreciation for dinner and that I made it inside my apartment without incident. I had enjoyed the evening. It was nice to go out again and to see that there was someone who wanted my company. Not like all the lies I had been fed by Joe during the time we were together.

Following the dinner, Bob asked me out again, and I accepted. He took me to a nice restaurant, and we had a great time. I did like Bob, and I enjoyed his company, but I was extremely cautious and would not allow myself to get sucked into any type of relationship. After several dates, when it became obvious Bob liked me, I told him a little bit of my past. I did not go into any detail, but it was clear that Bob was sympathetic, having struggled himself with a failed relationship.

Over time, Bob and I shared more of our struggles, and we would often read the Bible together. Bob was aware of my ongoing court battle and seemed to understand and be sympathetic, as he had his own issues over a land dispute with his ex-wife. Bob knew my boundaries, following the relationship and mistreatment from Joe, and respected these as they did not seem to be a huge hindrance to him. He sympathized and could not understand how someone could mistreat me or anyone else for that matter.

As my trial grew closer, one evening following a dinner with Bob, the stress became too much for me, and I had a bit of a meltdown over this ongoing character assassination. I cried unconsolably and asked the following questions: "This is the reason I survived, to be raked over the coals and my sins exposed to the whole world? Is this all there is? It is not worth it!"

Bob did not have a good reaction to this and decided it was best to distance himself from me. This just added insult to injury, as I again was humiliated and embarrassed at my behavior. I had held it together for so long, and then one vulnerable moment and it was all over between Bob and me. He no longer called or texted me. He would reply if I texted him, but it was not in my nature to pursue men, in general, as I was still very old school, and I thought that if Bob were interested, he would contact me. I prayed for the restoration of this relationship, but God had other plans.

As I mourned the loss of the relationship with Bob, the date of the trial loomed large, and once again, I was alone in my suffering. For the most part, my family and friends no longer wanted to hear anything about the trial. Some of the members of my church were supportive, as well as Joshua and my best friend, but I did not want to burden them, especially after what had happened with Bob. I knew this was a battle I must fight alone with only the Lord on my side. He was more than enough!

A few weeks before the trial, Mr. Gordon asked Joe's attorney if he would take a plea bargain but had replied that he would not even consider it. I met with Mr. Gordon on several occasions to prepare for the upcoming trial. He explained that I would likely be on the stand for one to two days and that as the trial continued, he would call the various witnesses as needed. This was going to be very exhausting, but it was too late to turn back now. I did not want to face Joe or his attorney, but it looked inevitable. I asked Mr. Gordon if I could hold something in my hand while testifying. He looked at me in a questioning manner and asked what it was that I wanted to hold. I showed him a bundle of small papers and explained that they were the promises of God. I handed them to him, and he immediately told me to hold on tight to these!

Several ladies from my church decided to attend the trial to support me. They put together a schedule so someone would be there the entire length of the trial. While I wanted the support, I was embarrassed at what they might hear and see. *I must get through this alone,* I thought to myself, as I had already brought so much shame to my family and myself. Even some family members did not want to hear any more about this. But these saints were undeterred.

Mr. Gordon had contacted about twenty or more witnesses who would be called to testify on my behalf, as needed. Most of these witnesses were co-workers or friends who witnessed Joe's behavior, especially after the assault. Many of these co-workers and friends were angry at me that they were called to testify and would call me to voice their thoughts. The sentiment was the same.

"I do not want to be involved in this situation. Why did you involve me?" I heard this complaint over and over. I apologized and explained that this monster needed to be put away to keep him from harming another innocent victim, and the fact that they had interacted with him was unfortunate. This did not do much for their attitude, but at least they agreed that they did not want him to harm anyone else. This was a tough time as many friends and co-workers did not want to have anything to do with me. Over time, this resolved for the most part, but to this day, there are still broken relationships that have not been mended.

THE PROCEEDING

Wednesday before the trial was to start, I received a phone call from Mr. Gordon explaining that Joe's attorney said Joe was interested in the plea bargain he had offered four weeks ago. Mr. Gordon said that he was prepared to go to trial and perhaps we should just say no, but then he shared with me what he was willing to offer. The terms of the plea bargain would include that Joe plead "no contest" to one of the two charges of assault with a deadly weapon, which in turn would require ten years of probation with the ankle monitor.

Mr. Gordon explained to me that during this ten-year period, if Joe got as much as a traffic ticket, this would automatically revoke the probation, and he would be required to serve the full twenty-year sentence with no chance of parole. He was not allowed in bars and could not consume alcohol or other drugs (legal or illegal) except under a doctor's care. He would be required to be drug tested at random times and would be required to see a probation officer for a monthly appointment. Joe was also required to surrender all his weapons.

Mr. Gordon told me that although this was not ideal, the way the system worked is that he could be out on good behavior in eighteen months if he was convicted and received the full ten-year sentence for the felony stalking count.

"This way, we can keep up with his whereabouts for ten years instead of eighteen months," he explained.

Mr. Gordon did not think Joe could stay out of trouble for ten years, so it may turn out to be a win-win situation. The decision was up to me.

THE END OR JUST THE BEGINNING?

If I accept this plea bargain and although there would be consequences, does Joe essentially walk out a free man?

I ultimately agreed to these terms, as there was no guarantee Joe would receive any punishment if we went to trial. As Mr. Gordon shared, at least I would know where he is for the next ten years, and I was optimistic Joe could not stay out of trouble for this length of time as the probation was fairly strict. I was also relieved that I would not have to go through the testimony and trial. Mr. Gordon explained to me that we were not out of the woods yet, as it would not be over until Joe came to the courts and signed all documents.

"Joe has the prerogative to change his mind at any moment, so nothing changes until the papers are signed. Joe must appear before the judge and sign the papers before Monday when the trial was to start, or the deal would be off," Mr. Gordon explained.

I understood this and anxiously awaited the return call to see if these terms would be accepted by Joe and his attorney. And most importantly, if they did accept the terms, would Joe show up to sign the agreement? Mr. Gordon called me back within an hour and told me that Joe and his attorney accepted the terms, and they were scheduled to come in to sign the papers that Friday morning. If all went according to the plan, then there would be no trial on Monday. It could all be over in less than forty-eight hours.

I was anxious to know the outcome on Friday, but also terrified that this gave Joe and his attorney time to regroup and change their mind. I do not think I slept at all during these two days, but I knew God would come through either way. He would give me strength to testify, if needed, or the courage to move on with my life on Friday. I held tightly to God's promise that He would never leave me.

"Be strong. Take courage. Don't be intimidated. Don't give them a second thought because God, your God, is striding ahead of you. He's right there with you. He won't let you down; he won't leave you."

DEUTERONOMY 31:6

THE IMPENDING JUDGEMENT

Friday morning came, and I briefly touched base with the district attorney's office to confirm that, indeed, the plea bargain was still on the table. Joshua was scheduled to meet with Mr. Gordon on Friday afternoon since he witnessed Joe's rage. The plan was still in the works for Joshua to come meet with Mr. Gordon, even though I explained to him that Joe may take the plea bargain. Joshua had laughed and told me that if the meeting got canceled, we could go for a celebratory lunch. I was so blessed to have Joshua's support.

Close to eleven that morning, Mr. Gordon called me and told me that Joe had indeed shown up and signed the documents with the court. It was over! Mr. Gordon also asked if I could accompany Joshua on his visit this afternoon, so he could explain things to both of us. I agreed and immediately phoned Joshua to tell him the news. Joshua confirmed that Mr. Gordon had also phoned him and requested we both come in for the scheduled meeting, despite the signing of the plea bargain. We were to meet at 1:30 that afternoon.

I felt excited and yet numb. After almost two years, would this finally be over, or would there be more to come? I did not know what Mr. Gordon wanted to tell us and why he requested that both Joshua and I meet with him. Joshua tried to calm my nerves, and said, "It is probably just explaining the paperwork to officially close out the case, nothing major."

I could not shake the feeling that something was terribly wrong. Maybe Joshua was right, and it was just the expected nervousness of months of living in anxiety. But I just kept getting the feeling that maybe this was not the end but just the beginning.

"You've kept track of my every toss and turn through the sleepless nights, each tear entered in your ledger, each ache written in your book."

PSALM 56:8

THE JIG IS UP

I pulled up to the district attorney's office and had to park in an area that seemed miles away and walk the several blocks to get to the building. I could not help but think how crowded the building was for a Friday afternoon. Joshua was waiting for me outside of the building, and we hugged for a moment.

Joshua asked, "You ready for this?"

I said, "I don't know, but let's go!"

We made our way into the courthouse to the floor where the district attorneys were housed, and almost immediately, Mr. Gordon came out and escorted Joshua and I back to his office. It was clear that I was apprehensive of what Mr. Gordon was going to say, but he took the opportunity to try to put me at ease.

"All of the paperwork is signed, and I have requested a copy for you, Ms. Powers," Mr. Gordon smiled and continued. "There are a number of things that you need to know regarding this case that I found out during the investigation. This is one of the reasons I had Joshua come with you, so he could hear these things also."

My heart was pounding as I looked over at Joshua, who reached out to pat my hand in an "everything will be okay" gesture.

"Yes, thank you for speaking with us," said Joshua. "We are ready to hear what you need to tell us."

I thought to myself that maybe Joshua was ready to hear the rest of the story, but I was not so sure I wanted to hear anything more. I did not think I could take any more shocking news.

Mr. Gordon started the conversation amidst the silence. "Ms. Powers, do you remember how you thought that Joe might have been poisoning you?"

"Yes," I immediately replied. "The protein shakes and coffee that he prepared for me daily, were what I guessed the sources of the poisoning might be," I added.

"We have found other witnesses who corroborated your story," Mr. Gordon continued. "I have a recorded testimony of another victim who barely escaped with her life. Let me play this for you and Joshua."

Joshua and I both sat in silence as Mr. Gordon started the recording. The interview was from a woman who Joe dated before meeting me as I recognized her name from Joe's stories. Joe told me she moved into his home with her teenage son after only knowing Joe for a few weeks. Joe had not specifically told me he killed them, but he challenged me to find them to ask what happens if you do not do as he requests. Praise God that she was alive, as well as her teenage son.

As I listened to her story unfold, her words sounded eerily familiar. She talked about how Joe insisted they get married and that he had lavished her with gifts, including a new car. She went on to explain that there were two occasions where she had to be hospitalized after drinking the protein shake and coffee, he prepared for her every morning. She became violently sick and required intravenous therapy to regain her strength. Of course, Joe was right there to help her and take care of her. He had told her not to worry about anything. He would make sure that no matter what happened, she and her son would be taken care of—forever. Joe forced her to drink more protein shakes when she came home, and within two weeks, she was back in the emergency room and admitted to the hospital. This time, she realized that she was being poisoned, and she had to get out, or she knew that she would die. She explained how she and her son planned an escape from his home.

Mr. Gordon stopped the interview and looked at Joshua and me. He spoke slowly with a slight quiver in his voice. "At this point in the interview, I realized that we no longer had an abuser on our hands, but we had a potential serial killer," he gulped.

"Please continue to listen." Mr. Gordon restarted the interview. The woman began to weep as she explained that Joe forced her to sell her car, and he had bought her a new one that was now in his name. She had no car and no way to escape. One day when Joe was gone, she took all her belongings, along with her son, and left in a taxi. She explained that she was terrified as she left. As she was leaving, Joe's daughter came out of the house. The woman explained that she listened in horror as Joe's daughter told her she was sorry for what happened and that she hoped she and her son were going to be all right and nothing bad would happen to them. Joe's daughter also said she admired her courage to leave before it was too late.

The woman on the interview went into hysterics. She cried thinking what Joe's daughter must have lived through. Likely years of unspeakable horror but she could not turn her own father in to the authorities. The woman then described the barrage of threats that ensued when Joe arrived home to find her gone, but by this time, she was in hiding and prayed Joe would not find her.

As the interview concluded, the woman must have realized that Joe had done something terrible or succeeded in killing someone if the district attorney was contacting her about him. She cried out in remorse for not reporting him to law enforcement.

"This man is a killer," she cried. "He killed his wife and then tried to kill me. Did he kill someone else also? I could have prevented this, and I did nothing because I was too afraid."

She then explained that she had moved out of the area and changed her phone number, so Joe would not find her. Mr. Gordon explained that he could not divulge any information to her at the time as it could jeopardize the case, but he promised her that he would be in touch again. Joshua and I sat in disillusionment. Neither of us could believe what we had just heard.

Mr. Gordon continued, "There is more."

Joshua and I sat in horror as Mr. Gordon explained to us what the expert in body art and piercings had concluded regarding the tattoos on Joe's body.

"Essentially, these tattoos are not gang-related, but Joe was commemorating or marking a remembrance of his victims." Mr. Gordon said.

He then showed me pictures of Joe's shaved head. "Do you recall seeing this tattoo, Ms. Powers?" Mr. Gordon asked.

"No, never," I replied in horror at the series of numbers on the back of Joe's head.

Mr. Gordon explained that it was the date his wife had died, and Joe had marked himself as a remembrance or reminder of this day.

"He did not have this tattoo when I met him," I replied. "He had shaved his head, but there were no numbers there. I would have noticed this."

Mr. Gordon asked me, "Are you sure about this?" as he wrote down information in his notebook.

"Yes, absolutely," I said.

There were other pictures of tattoos on Joe's body that Mr. Gordon showed and then explained to me their meaning according to the expert's analysis. Some of them I recognized but most were new, and I had never seen them.

"We believe that there are more victims out there, based on the tattoo markings," Mr. Gordon explained.

I was overwhelmed and feeling very weak at this point. Joshua grabbed my hand as if to say we were going to be okay now. I think I was going into shock when Mr. Gordon finally finished with his explanation of the markings on Joe's body.

As Joshua and I looked over at each other as in a "let's go" gesture, Mr. Gordon said, "There is one more thing."

We both sat back and tried to relax to hear more of the terrifying tales. Mr. Gordon explained that he would be having a police escort for a while, as well as his wife and small children. There was a police officer stationed at his home also.

"What?" I cried out, "Why?"

"During the hearing this morning in front of the judge, Joe was taking pictures of me." Mr. Gordon explained. "I was talking to the judge, and one of the attorneys, who was waiting in the courtroom for another case, kept motioning to me to stop speaking with the judge as he needed to tell me something. I thought this was very strange as you don't interrupt a conversation with a judge especially when you are waiting to present your client. I finally acknowledged his gesture as he would not let it go.

The attorney came forward and explained to the judge and me that this defendant was taking photos of us. The judge burned in anger and demanded to see Joe's phone and saw that it was true. The judge admonished Joe and took his phone away. Joe tried to explain that it was an accident, but the judge was hearing none of it. The judge sternly warned Joe that when (not if) he saw him again, he would revoke all sentences, and he would spend the next twenty years locked up."

Mr. Gordon did not appear to be overly upset about the incident, but I was clearly shaken up as well as Joshua. I was horrified feeling that I had put Mr. Gordon, his wife, and children in danger. I apologized over and over, but Mr. Gordon smiled and said, "This is what I do, and my wife is used to it—I guess as best as you can get used to it—but she knew this when she married me, so she is good."

I felt terrible for causing his family trouble.

As he looked at me, I was on the verge of tears, he said, "Ms. Powers, you are a hero. You stopped a potential serial killer in his tracks. We will get him for this. Don't you worry."

I certainly did not feel like a hero, more like a failure. As Joshua and I got up to leave, I finally summoned up the courage to address Mr. Gordon for the last time. "Mr. Gordon, everyone at this office has been so kind and supportive of me, especially you. What can I ever do to repay you?"

Mr. Gordon smiled and said, "You really want to repay me?"

"Yes, of course," I said. Mr. Gordon then looked directly at me and said, "Tell your story."

It felt like Mr. Gordon was not speaking but rather the voice of God telling me to do this.

Mr. Gordon added, "Take a little time off, but when you are ready, tell your story."

"I will, I promise you," I mumbled through the tears as I left the office.

On the way out of the building, I was greeted by other members of the district attorney's office, who thanked me for my bravery. *I was not brave at all*, I thought, as I passed through the hallways into the elevator banks. Joshua and I exited the courthouse in silence. Finally, when we arrived outside of the building, Joshua looked at me and asked if I was okay.

"I don't know."

He concurred the same feelings. "Well, I love you, Mom. We will talk soon," Joshua said as he started to walk to his car.

"Yes, talk soon," my voice trailed off as he disappeared around the corner.

It was a strange parting for Joshua and me, but I figured he was dealing with the trauma in his own way. I slowly walked the seemingly endless blocks to my car, but I did not even notice the distance now, as I seemed to be in a state of shock and disbelief. When I finally got to my car, I opened the door and climbed in. I locked the door and started the engine, but I was frozen. I could not stop the flood of tears that immediately ensued. *What just happened?* I thought to myself. It was unbelievable.

The months and years of suffering came pouring out like a fountain. How could I have been so blind and put myself and others in such danger? All I wanted was love. But then a great truth overtook me. What about all of Joe's previous or current victims? Mr. Gordon said I was a hero for having the courage to expose him, but I do not see this as a victory. People are dead because of this monster, and he is out there free, primed, and ready for the next kill. Did I really stop him or just slow him down? These thoughts flooded my mind, and it was impossible to think clearly.

"Oh Lord, please help me! This is too much to bear," I cried.

God's message was clear to me at that moment. "Hope, be present, and be alert for the Lord your God is about to do a new thing!"

"Forget about what's happened; don't keep going over old history. Be alert, be present. I'm about to do something brand-new..."

ISAIAH 43:18-19

I felt the presence of the Lord, and His still small voice continued, "I have plans for you, Hope. I have called you by name. Follow me and do as I ask!"

"Me, why would you call me Lord? I am not worthy!" I replied.

I felt the Lord say, "No one is worthy. I put the punishment of the world's sin on my Son at the cross, so do not fall victim to the lies of the enemy. And it was not a question, Hope. Now, dry your eyes and let's get going."

> "...Don't be afraid, I've redeemed you. I've called your name. You're mine. When you're in over your head, I'll be there with you. When you're in rough waters, you will not go down. When you're between a rock and a hard place, it won't be a dead end—"
>
> ISAIAH 43:1-2

I immediately dried my tears and started the drive home. I felt God's love give me new hope for a new beginning. Perhaps this was the beginning and not the end. I was not sure of anything anymore except for God's amazing love for me. I knew that eventually, the fog would clear, but for now, I was secure in the arms of my Savior, knowing He had plans for me.

> "We don't yet see things clearly. We're squinting in a fog, peering through a mist. But it won't be long before the weather clears and the sun shines bright! We'll see it all then, see it all as clearly as God sees us, knowing him directly just as he knows us!"
>
> 1 CORINTHIANS 13:12

CHAPTER 8

WHAT REMAINS

"...Don't be afraid, I've redeemed you. I've called your name. You're mine.
When you're in over your head, I'll be there with you. When you're in rough
waters, you will not go down. When you're between a rock and a hard place, it
won't be a dead end— Because I am God, your personal God, The Holy of Israel,
your Savior. I paid a huge price for you..."
Isaiah 43:1-3

There is life and healing after domestic violence—it is not a lifelong sentence. No matter what you have done, you did not deserve this. I have repeated this over and over throughout the book, so I hope by now it might begin to sink in. This does not mean that everything will be wonderful going forward, as I have experienced true brokenness, hit rock bottom, and still, at times, continue to battle for my freedom from judgement and sin. But there is hope and redemption following a traumatic event. Remember, the Lord paid a huge price for each of us, and we are His. He will never let us go.

GOD PREFERS TO USE BROKEN PEOPLE

I was having coffee with my pastor, shortly after the assault and separation, and was telling him the blow-by-blow details of all that had happened. As I talked, I realized it must have seemed like a strangely wild and weird tale. I stopped talking and immediately felt shame and guilt overcome me.

"What is it, Hope?" my pastor asked.

"I do not think I can continue with the details," I said. "I am broken—I think beyond repair. I am sorry."

During those few minutes, I suddenly realized the words I had just spoken. How could I be any good to anyone now, as I was so broken? The sorrow of this moment almost led me to tears. My pastor started to smile. I thought this was unusual as this was not the response I expected.

"Don't you know God prefers to use broken people, Hope?" he said almost at a giggle now.

"What?" I chimed back.

"Sure," he added. "Do you not remember the story in the Bible of the woman who anointed Jesus's feet with an expensive perfume?"

"Yes, of course," I said, "she was chastised by the disciples who were around and told that she could have sold that perfume for a year's wages and donated that money to the poor."

"Yes," he said," that is right, but you know that the vessel had to be broken for the perfume to flow to Jesus's feet. Don't you see that you must be broken so all the good stuff can be let out. If you remain an unbroken vessel, no one will know what is inside."

"I understand," I sheepishly smiled.

Upon hearing my pastor's words, I was reminded of a memory from years back when I attended a different church in another town. The pastor's wife sang a beautiful song about this. It is funny how the enemy kept this thought under wraps until now. The words to this song still resonate with me today, as I can envision the vessel being "broken and spilled out" with the fragrance filling the air. I can see the truth in the analogy my pastor was trying to relate to me. I am certainly "spilled out" and felt I created a mess. But the one thing I have come to realize is that God uses messes.

Once I realized this truth, the stories of the heroes of faith started coming back to me. Over and over, I was reminded of ordinary people like Abraham, Jacob, Joseph, and even Rahab, a prostitute who was in the bloodline of Jesus. They were all broken in some form, and yet God used them in miraculous ways. *I was certainly broken,* I thought to myself, so I should qualify as a prime candidate for God to use me. But not everyone saw me in this light, as I will discuss further in a later section. My brokenness was on display for the world to see, and some of my so-called friends and disapproving coworkers smelled fresh blood. They would come in droves to continue to persecute. I was rejected over and over. This added to my brokenness.

ARE YOU BROKEN-HEARTED?

If you answered yes, then this is good news. I can imagine how you might be feeling because I have been there too. Please do not think I have lost my mind when I tell you that being broken is good news. God is in this with you, and He is in the fixing business! It took me months, if not years, to realize my broken heart was a blessing. It is so easy to be passive with God when all is going well, but give me a crisis and I am on my knees crying out for help. I hate to admit this, but I would say this is true for most of us. I do not think it is intentional, but I have noticed that sometimes the bigger the problem, the closer I am to God. If I had not gone through all this suffering, where would I be now? God had to get my attention somehow, and maybe He is trying to get yours.

In the parable of the wedding banquet in Matthew 22, Jesus illustrates that God's kingdom is like a wedding banquet thrown by a king for his son. The king's servants send out the invitations, but many made excuses as to why they could not come. Fearing that no one would show for the wedding banquet, the king told his servants to send out the invitations to anyone who they saw regardless of status or class. The banquet was soon filled. As the king viewed the guests, he noticed one was not properly dressed for the occasion and kicked him out. The guest was stunned at this. This is what Jesus meant when He said, "Many get invited; only a few make it." (Matthew 22:14).

The Lord will do what He needs to do to get your attention, as it is not His will that any should perish (2 Peter 3:9). If you continue to refuse His calling, you will end up like the guest who was not properly dressed for the banquet and be asked to leave. God will meet you right where you are. He is inviting you to the banquet. It does not matter that your heart is broken, and you think you are broken beyond repair. Trust Him and see what He has in store for you. You will be amazed!

"Heart-shattered lives ready for love don't for a moment escape God's notice."

PSALM 51:17

BATTLE FOR FREEDOM

Have you ever been on a diet and found it hard to resist food you know you should not eat? The struggle is real. Your brain knows you should eat the right foods for your health, but that chocolate bar is calling your name and is so tempting. The struggle for our true freedom in Christ is also an ongoing battle we must fight for daily, even though we may not recognize the urgency in this fight. Each day we must choose for ourselves who we will serve, as Joshua 24:15 states. I encourage you to choose to fight for your freedom today and not return to slavery. The path can be a slippery slope, no doubt, and one that is easy to fall back into because it is familiar. Choosing each day to walk in freedom with Christ is worth it, even though it might be difficult at times.

After the assault, I struggled with self-esteem, self-worth, self-respect, and any other word related to self. It sounds like I was a little self-absorbed, which could be true, but after going through a traumatic event, there is a great deal of internal recovery work that must be done. As I described earlier, I cried out to God daily, saying, "You saved me for this? I would have rather died."

At the time, that was a true reflection of how I felt. What I have come to know is that as long as I am alive, there will always be a struggle of sorts, but God is faithful in His Word and sets me right back up on the path I should go.

> "He heals the heartbroken and bandages their wounds. He counts the stars and assigns each a name. Our Lord is great, with limitless strength; we'll never comprehend what he knows and does. God puts the fallen on their feet again and pushes the wicked into the ditch."
>
> PSALM 147:3-6

If you are a survivor of domestic violence or abuse, know that you are not alone in your struggle. Each day, month, and year, the struggle gets less and less as you allow God to heal your broken heart. Sometimes certain settings, places, or incidents send me right back to those days of abuse. I have run into people from the past who question me about Joe or new friends who perhaps want to go to mine and Joe's old hangouts. I have gotten better at dealing with these situations, but they never completely go away. I am thankful that even on the hardest days, I can reflect on the goodness of God. The struggle is real, but so is my God!

BECOMING A CRUSADER

Crusader: someone who makes a determined effort to achieve or stop something because of their strong beliefs.[5]

Crusade: a concerted effort or vigorous movement for a cause or against an abuse.[6]

This is the direction I began as a start for healing. I learned all the statistics and even attended the National Coalition Against Domestic Violence Conference as a guest survivor on scholarship. I was determined to make a difference even if it was only for one person. In my own way, I was going to become a crusader against domestic violence.

We are all called to tell our stories as a testament to how Jesus has worked in our lives, so others can take courage from our stories, no matter how small or unimportant your difficulties may seem. Abuse of any kind is serious. It tears apart families, ruins lives, and can have horrific outcomes if the violence escalates. I encourage you to talk about your difficulties, even if it is a one-on-one conversation with a trusted individual.

Get help! Seek the advice of a counselor. After you have received help, you can also become a crusader and tell others how you have overcome through Jesus Christ. There is something therapeutic and healing in talking about your experiences and in helping others.

THE RISING JUDGEMENT

The rising judgment encompasses two variables: 1) the judgment you put on yourself for the mistakes you have made and 2) the judgment of others. These are exceedingly difficult obstacles to overcome. Having lived in abusive environments for a good portion of my life, I would say that these are the two hardest to overcome. You can recover from physical wounds and trauma, but long after these scars are healed, the effects of the emotional, spiritual, and mental abuse will remain.

Getting Past My Own Judgement

How can I forgive myself for my past sins and bad choices whose consequences I must deal with currently? How can I overcome my circumstances and be victorious again? Both questions seem insurmountable in my own strength. I am not worthy of God's love, much less His mercy. The good news is that none of us are. Even the "holier than thou" folks fall into the category of sinner.

> "For all have sinned and fall short of the glory of God."
>
> ROMANS 3:23 NIV

I praise God every day that He delivered me out of the hands of this evil monster and back into His fellowship and that He provides me the strength to live a victorious life. I often must take a step back and realize God rescued and saved me for a purpose. It was not His intent that I stay in the abusive situation. Instead, He turned my circumstances around to reveal MORE of His GLORY! Hallelujah!

While I still struggle with self-judgment, I often feel the Holy Spirit whisper in my ear, "I have no idea of these sins you speak of, Hope. I have forgiven you, and you have been washed whiter than snow, and you stand unscathed in my presence."

This is hard to comprehend in my finite brain, but over time, I am beginning to accept this more and more.

> "With the arrival of Jesus, the Messiah, that fateful dilemma
> is resolved. Those who enter into Christ's being-here-for-us no
> longer have to live under a continuous, low-lying black cloud. A
> new power is in operation."
>
> ROMANS 8:1

I no longer must live under this black cloud of guilt and shame but yield to the new power in my life with Jesus Christ. If you have suffered abuse of any kind, whether as a young child or as an adult, you do not have to live under the weight of guilt and shame. Regardless of your circumstances, you did not deserve to be abused.

I know this is sometimes hard to accept as your abuser will tell you it is all your fault, and when this is "beaten" into your head repeatedly, you start to believe it. As I have written numerous times throughout the various chapters of this book, Jesus is calling us to freedom from guilt and shame. Jesus died for these very things, so all you need to do is ask for His forgiveness, accept it, and start to enjoy your freedom. I know it is easier said than done, but with His help, you can get beyond the sufferings of surviving domestic violence and abuse.

Getting Past the Judgement of Others

This has been one of the hardest areas for me to overcome—getting past the judgment of others and essentially ignoring their comments. I want to isolate myself and not associate with anyone outside of my very intimate circle of friends and family who I feel that I can trust. Sometimes even in this intimate circle, there are those I must keep at a distance, as their comments can sometimes be condescending and hurtful.

Since this incident, I have always tried to live by the principle of uplifting others and watching what I say so my words will not drag them down. Words wound deeply. You can heal from the physical, but the emotional blows take much longer. The Bible states that death and life are in the power of the tongue (Proverbs 18:21), and I have found this to be so true. What we say to others can take a toll on their well-being and walk with Christ. We as Christians should walk as Jesus walked (1 John 2:6). I cannot think of anything worse than surviving unspeakable acts of evil and horror, and then to be criticized, judged, or worse—completely ignored by friends, family, and even looked down on by members of the church.

"Watch the way you talk. Let nothing foul or dirty come out of your mouth. Say only what helps, each word a gift."

EPHESIANS 4:29

During the trial and aftermath, it became hard for some of my closest confidants to continue to support me. These confidants thought I should let this matter go and not be engaged with the district attorney or any court battles. I had come too far to take this approach, as I often explained. At this point, I decided not to speak a word about Joe, the district attorney, or the court case. This decision was heartbreaking, in that I could no longer rely on their support, but I understood that this situation was intense.

This scenario repeated itself as the case went on for months and months. Sometimes, I would get the "holier than thou" attitude as someone would echo the sentiment that this was taking too much of a toll on my life, and out of their "great concern" for me, they did not want to be a part of my ongoing self-destruction. So they would no longer continue to engage in the conversation. They would use my weight loss as a point of their case. My reaction to this statement was intense, but only in my thoughts—*This man tried to destroy my life, and I am trying to gain my life back, but you see this as destruction and not what he did?*

In reality, I said nothing. I would just choose to no longer burden them with my "drama." I built up walls, thick and high walls. I believe that for most of the "holier than thou" crowd, it was an inconvenience and something they did not want to acknowledge or think about, so it was easier to write me off as being self-destructive for wanting justice than to face their own fears. And who knows, statistically speaking, maybe I was getting a little too close to home for their liking.

"Don't pick on people, jump on their failures, criticize their
faults—unless, of course, you want the same treatment. That
critical spirit has a way of boomeranging. It's easy to see a
smudge on your neighbor's face and be oblivious to the ugly
sneer on your own. Do you have the nerve to say, 'Let me
wash your face for you,' when your own face is distorted by
contempt?"

MATTHEW 7:1-4

For a time, my life was full of despair and anguish. Most of the friendships
lost were never reconciled, and I suppose as many would echo, "these
were not true friends," but the lasting pain does not subside. It flares its
ugly head again when I am overlooked, left out, or not invited to be a
part of the group. "It is awkward to be around her," I have heard others
whisper about me when my back was turned. It has been several years
now since the trial was over, and I have moved on with my life. "What
is awkward?" I wanted to ask, but I remained silent.

"So where does that leave you when you criticize a brother?
And where does that leave you when you condescend to a sister?
I'd say it leaves you looking pretty silly—or worse. Eventually,
we're all going to end up kneeling side by side in the place of
judgment, facing God. Your critical and condescending ways
aren't going to improve your position there one bit."

ROMANS 14:10

I often feel invisible or different than others, no matter where I go. The
feeling that I do not fit in is overwhelming.

> "The fear of human opinion disables; trusting in God protects you from that."
>
> PROVERBS 29:25

But Jesus always reminds me that He did not fit in either, and maybe, being invisible is all right for now, as we believe not in what is seen but what is unseen.

> "The things we see now are here today, gone tomorrow. But the things we can't see now will last forever."
>
> 2 CORINTHIANS 4:18

With all this said, there have been an elite group of people, I like to call them "the saints," who have been by my side throughout this whole ordeal. They took a call at any hour of the day or night and would drop on their knees to pray with me. I do not think I would have made it through the long nights without them. Then of course, there is my best friend, Mary, who no matter what, she is there and never imparts judgement.

Joshua has also been a huge support, and even in the dark times, he seems to have an understanding without judgment. Caleb and Rachel have been by my side as well, always willing to listen or help me when I needed it. I am eternally grateful to all of those who supported me, and I hold no grudge or ill-will toward those who could not continue with their support. It has not been easy. I believe everyone must make their own choices, and with those choices come consequences. By stepping away, they have missed the most important and best part, the end, or should I say the new beginning?

AWAKENING NEW HOPE

I often think of how fitting and perfect my name, Hope, is for my life circumstances. I would have never imagined how a new Hope (both literally and figuratively) might have appeared those years ago as I looked at my reflection in the mirror. I now look in the mirror through the eyes of my Savior, Jesus Christ, and ask Him if I can see my vision, not my reflection. All hope is not lost; it has been found. If you have suffered or still suffer from domestic abuse or violence, there is hope no matter your circumstances.

How many nights will I cry myself to sleep? Will this pain never end? I often asked myself these questions, especially when I was alone night after night. I felt like I could not go on, but I did. I kept going, not because it was easy but because I had no choice. I often lamented each day to Joshua when he asked how my day went that the rapture had not occurred, so I would wait another day.

Joshua's comment was always the same, "I am sorry, Momma."

Eventually, the tears began to dry, and I was able to sleep and eat again. It took a long time, but I began to feel as if I was going to make it through. I held tightly to God's promises.

"The nights of crying your eyes out give way to days of laughter."

PSALM 30:5

In some respects, I am still waiting for the days of laughter, but at least the nights of crying have subsided for the most part. Although I am still alone, I move forward with God's purpose for my life. I have experienced many blessings and saw God work in ways I could have never imagined. For this, I am eternally grateful. I am not sure I have seen the last tear fall, but I trust and believe there are days of laughter coming soon, and this gives me continued hope.

> "You're blessed when the tears flow freely.
> Joy comes with the morning."
>
> LUKE 6:21

I add that being alone is not bad compared to living in constant fear and abuse. Over time, you get used to it and actually come to enjoy it. I often joke with my friends that I never have to argue with anyone about the temperature setting or what to have for dinner. It took me almost two years following the assault to be able to relax enough to realize that I needed to thank God for providing me with a safe home to live in. It was a strange realization, but one that many people take for granted. Although there are occasions when I am extremely cautious of my surroundings, I am thankful to the Lord that I can live in peace now without constant fear and looking over my shoulder.

HE MAKES ALL THINGS NEW

In 2020, the world was hit with a pandemic. My life, as well as the lives of everyone around me, changed. We were all placed in lockdown for many months while we watched in horror as the staggering case numbers, hospitalizations, and death count rose. This pandemic lasted well into 2021, and just as we thought we had turned the corner at the end of 2020, a new deadly variant of the virus emerged. At the beginning of every year, I write my new year's resolutions and select a theme word for that year. For 2021, I selected the word "transition" as I embraced the biblical principle that God makes all things new.

"He'll wipe every tear from their eyes. Death is gone for good—tears gone, crying gone, pain gone—all the first order of things gone." The Enthroned continued, "Look! I'm making everything new. Write it all down—each word dependable and accurate."

REVELATION 21:4–5

As the year 2021 went on, I decided to leave my secure office job and take on a new job working in a hospital. This seemed like a huge leap of faith during a pandemic, but I prayed diligently for this position and cried out to the Lord to have His will done in my life. As requested, the Lord intervened, and I was selected. Almost immediately, I knew something was wrong. Before I started to work, the director who hired me left the hospital for another job. *Strange,* I thought, *but I guess these things happen.* As the months wore on, the job became increasingly stressful largely because a co-worker was verbally abusive and just downright mean to me. She had run off my main contact in the department, and now she had me in her sights.

Again, I cried out to God, "Why? I thought this was where you wanted me!"

His reply was the same time after time, "You are right where I want you. Just wait."

The abuse continued and escalated. When a new director was hired, I shared with him the stress and abuse I was under due to this co-worker. I had broken away from my old job, where people knew my story, and I was comfortable. This cannot be what God had intended for me. Finally, when I cried out to God in desperation, after calculating how I might survive if I just quit, He gave me a different answer.

"Hope, look at the job offerings now," the Lord gently spoke to me.

As I eagerly looked at the job site, the first job I saw was a position in a Christian ministry. The position matched my skills perfectly, and I had been a huge supporter of this ministry for years.

"Thank you, Lord!" I cried.

Then the doubt rolled in. How can I work in ministry with my background? They will not allow anyone to work in this ministry who has been divorced, much less divorced more than one time! I am too big of a sinner.

"APPLY!" was almost audible as it came directly from the voice of the Lord.

"Okay, okay, I am applying," I smiled and said to myself.

I quickly got my resume together and sent it to the email address listed on the job description. It was then I noticed that the job had been posted for more than ten days now. Another let down moment as I was sure it was too late, and they already had someone in mind for the position.

"Have faith!" the Lord whispered in my ear.

Within four hours, I received an email confirming that my resume had been sent to the hiring manager, and within twenty-four hours, I had received a notice that the hiring manager wanted to interview me. I love the way that the Lord exceeds our expectations.

> "God can do anything, you know—far more than you could ever imagine or guess or request in your wildest dreams!"
>
> EPHESIANS 3:20

The Lord truly has blessed me beyond measure, and YES, I got the job! Me, the rejected, sinful, and beaten down me, now works in full-time ministry for my Lord. This experience makes me think of the story of Joseph in Genesis 37. The Lord needed to get Joseph to Egypt, but how? We all know the story of the many diversions that Joseph encountered on his way to Egypt. It was not an easy trip being sold into slavery, accused of rape, going to jail, and then forgotten are just a few of Joseph's experiences in getting to Egypt. But in the end, God placed Joseph exactly where he needed him to be, according to His perfect will, so that he could save God's chosen people from starvation in a time of famine.

> "As for you, you meant evil against me, but God meant it for good, to bring it about that many people should be kept alive, as they are today."
>
> GENESIS 50:20 ESV

While my story is not near as dramatic as Joseph's, God often uses diversions to get us to His desired destination for our lives. I use this story to describe the new hope granted to me in my life following this traumatic event. This was truly a year of transition for me. Domestic violence and abuse should not be a life sentence or have a death sentence. We are so much more than that to our Lord. Although it took several years, I had been ready for this transition. I invite you to consider making this transition into the freedom Jesus has promised. Awaken a new hope!

WE ARE MORE THAN CONQUERORS!

I am sure that many of you are thinking, sure, that worked for you, but it will not or cannot work for me. You do not know my full situation. I would encourage you to think about the teachings of Paul when he tells the church in Rome (and us) that we are more than conquerors. I know that every circumstance is different, and although I cannot fathom what anyone else has gone through or may still be going through, one thing I do know is we can overcome by God's amazing grace and mercy.

> "So, what do you think? With God on our side like this, how can we lose? If God didn't hesitate to put everything on the line for us, embracing our condition and exposing himself to the worst by sending his own Son, is there anything else he wouldn't gladly and freely do for us?"
>
> ROMANS 8:31-32

FOLLOW GOD'S INSTRUCTIONS

No matter what you think or what others think about your circumstances, you should always follow God's instructions for your life. While I cannot tell you the choices I made escaping domestic violence would be the right choices for you, there is help available, but it must start with God. How does this work? What if I do not hear from God, or it is not clear what I should do? I have asked these same questions in the past, and sometimes I even question God if He hears my cries, even though I know He does. Here is a simple model I follow that I believe can help in first seeking God's will for your life and then following what He asks you to do.

First, pray, and then pray again (and again). 1 Thessalonians 5:17 tells us to pray without ceasing or continually. In other words, you can never pray too much. In part one of my story, I have a short interjection where I discuss prayer. I added that section because although I did pray about my circumstances, I was still deceived because I did not wait on the Lord for an answer. I took matters into my own hands thinking I was doing God's will, but I was deceived. The enemy stalks us day and night like a lion ready to pounce when we least expect it.

"Keep a cool head. Stay alert. The Devil is poised to pounce, and would like nothing better than to catch you napping. Keep your guard up."

1 PETER 5:8

Second, know what God says on a matter by studying His Word daily. When you are faced with a threat from the enemy, it is important to know what God has already spoken on the matter. For example, when Jesus was in the wilderness and tempted by Satan, He resisted by quoting God's Word back to Satan. If we are immersed in studying God's Word daily, we can learn how to become stronger in defeating the enemy.

Friends, going to church every Sunday, which is a good thing, is not enough to be prepared for the ensuing battle! The enemy is out to kill, steal, and destroy. Jesus came to give us life, but we must know the words that defend against the evils that are present to take our souls.

> "A thief is only there to steal and kill and destroy. I came so they can have real and eternal life, more and better life than they ever dreamed of."
>
> JOHN 10:10

As a bonus, reading from God's Word daily renews your strength as His Word never returns void. I love the way The Message version of the Bible phrases Isaiah 55:11, "So will the words that come out of my mouth not come back empty-handed." You will never be left empty handed after reading God's Word.

Third, listen to the still small voice He puts in your heart and obey Him. If you do not hear the voice, then wait until you do. He will speak truth to your heart. In 1 Kings 19:11-14, Elijah is listening for God's voice. God's voice was not in the hurricane or earthquake but in a gentle and quiet whisper. We need to be patient and still to hear His voice. Focus your prayers on asking Him to speak to you.

> "…A hurricane wind ripped through the mountains and shattered the rocks before God, but God wasn't to be found in the wind; after the wind an earthquake, but God wasn't in the earthquake; and after the earthquake fire, but God wasn't in the fire; and after the fire a gentle and quiet whisper."
>
> 1 KINGS 19:11-12

After my experience, I do not always trust that I hear His voice and not my own, or worse, that of the enemy. I pray for ongoing discernment of His voice, but I also ask God to let me know if this is Him speaking or me making up something so that I will know beyond a shadow of a doubt that it is Him. In other words, give me a sign it is You, God. He is faithful and always lets me know. I just have to be patient.

BLESSED TO BE A BLESSING

After all I have endured and survived, I have been overwhelmingly blessed by God. I do not deserve this blessing by any means, but I remember the kindness and compassion that was poured out to me during my times of struggle and need. Part of my healing came when I decided to pay the kindness and compassion forward and stop focusing on my pain. Although we all have unmet needs of some type, we can be a support to each other if we are willing.

In my pursuit of "paying it forward," I decided to sign up to be a mentor to a first-grade child who came from a single-parent home. There were five siblings living with this child, and the mom tried her best to scrape out a living to support the six children. The child was a discipline problem, clearly brought on by a lack of attention. I agreed to meet with this child once a week for an hour. The teacher would often email me or call me to give me an update on the child's behavior for the week, so we could talk about it during our time together.

Over the months of meetings, I brought the child gifts and shared the gospel. I was even invited to participate in the Valentine's Day party as this child's special guest. Several of the other children's mothers were there to help celebrate, and I stood proudly as my child was able to show me all the work that had been ongoing in the classroom. I even got to read a story to the entire class. The experience was one I will never forget. Shortly after the party, I got word that my child had moved. I was saddened, but the teacher explained to me that the mother had gotten a better job and was able to provide a safer and more secure place for her family to live. What a blessing! I often think about this child and continue to pray for her. Maybe I laid a seed that someone else will come alongside and water in this child's life.

This is just another example of how I began my journey of healing. I am sure this child benefited from my presence, but to be honest, I was blessed so much more. It is funny how God works like that. I was able to stop focusing on my problems for an hour a week and focus on this child, one of God's most precious creations. I consider it a privilege to have been placed in this situation, even though it was short-lived. The Lord truly blessed me, so I could bless this small little child.

> "One day children were brought to Jesus in the hope that he would lay hands on them and pray over them. The disciples shooed them off. But Jesus intervened: 'Let the children alone, don't prevent them from coming to me. God's kingdom is made up of people like these.'"
>
> MATTHEW 19:13-15

I envision that God sees me as a child, dressed in white, with flowers in my hair, running by a pond of still water. Even though I am grown, I am still a child in His eyes. I believe God sees all His children this way. His precious children, pure as snow and shining bright as the sun. Despite our faults, we are forgiven through His infinite grace and mercy.

INVITATION TO FREEDOM

"He heals the heartbroken and bandages their wounds. God puts the fallen on their feet again and pushes the wicked into the ditch."
Psalm 147:3, 6

HOW CAN I LIVE MY BEST LIFE?

I often get asked how I got past this season of my life. I guess the best answer is that I have not gotten past this part of my life but instead have learned to live with my newfound freedom by walking every day with Jesus, my Lord and Savior.

"My counsel is this: Live freely, animated and motivated by God's Spirit..."

GALATIANS 5:16

I often have thought *if only I could return to the beginning and redo this part of my life*, but I know it is not possible. However, I believe the Lord allowed me to experience this season and saved me from certain death, so I may help others find their freedom. I know I do not have all the answers, but what I do know is with God, all things are possible (Matthew 19:26).

> "Jesus looked hard at them and said, "No chance at all if you think you can pull it off yourself. Every chance in the world if you trust God to do it."
>
> MATTHEW 19:26

There was no way I had a chance to survive, but with God's help, there was every chance in the world. PRAISE HIM!

My life today is much different than before I went through this trauma. I have managed to gain my health back, although, on occasion, I still suffer from the pain in my arms as I am sure there was damage done to the tissue. The markers for autoimmune disease are no longer present in my blood. I have large scars and slight discoloration from multiple surgeries on my wrist. I often have stiffness in my wrist as there has been a type of arthritis that has developed, often seen with a crushing injury.

Although I believe I will one day be completely healed of this stiffness and pain, this stands as a constant reminder to me of my turbulent past and how the Lord rescued me. Other physical injuries have healed, but I often feel that I still suffer from a broken heart and crushed spirit. I remember the Lord is close to the broken hearted and saves those who are crushed in spirit, or as The Message translation states it:

"If your heart is broken, you'll find God right there; if you're kicked in the gut, he'll help you catch your breath."

PSALM 34:18

I think we can all relate to how it feels to be kicked in the gut, at least from an emotional standpoint. The emotional aspect of this is probably the worst, but I hold steadfast to God's promise as He makes a way in the wilderness and put streams in the wasteland of my life.

"Forget the former things; do not dwell on the past. See, I am doing a new thing! Now it springs up; do you not perceive it? I am making a way in the wilderness and streams in the wasteland."

ISAIAH 43:18-19 NIV

THE AFTERMATH FOR OTHERS

Joshua moved to the city and got an excellent job. He has recently married a wonderful girl who treats him well. We rarely speak of those years anymore, as Joshua has gotten on with his life. Joshua is talented in the arts and has written a musical about my story. In the musical, Joshua takes away Joe's voice, and at the end, I am given the choice of life or death for Joe. It is a powerful and moving piece that I hope one day I can see performed live. God's goodness is everlasting.

My oldest son, Caleb, as well as my daughter, Rachel, have both moved away for their jobs. As I see my sweet little grandchildren grow from tiny infants into beautiful young children who love the Lord, I am so thankful to God for preserving their lives and keeping them safe from this madman.

Mary is still my best friend, and I visit her and Dan often. I am so thankful I have these friends as constants in my life. They have been a blessing and helped me through thick and thin. I still travel with them from time to time but always alone.

Mike Fuller, the security manager who helped me escape, retired and moved to another state. I have not stayed in touch, but I will always be grateful to him and the family that hid me for their help that fateful day. I pray this book will, in some small way, pay it forward to them.

I have not been in touch with Mr. Gordon, the district attorney, since our last meeting, where he revealed Joe was a potential serial killer. My prayer is that wherever he is now, he will know I have finally told my story. I believe he would smile at this.

The couple in Reno were not left unscathed by this encounter. The wife attempted suicide twice and left me a bizarre but apologetic text message prior to each attempt. She had said in her text messages that she could not forgive herself for the events of that fateful night. I tried to call her numerous times, but she would not take my calls. I wish I could tell her that I forgave her long ago, and it is not her fault. God is still on the throne, and she should come back to Him, as He is calling her into freedom from her guilt.

After the trial was over, Bob wanted to reconcile our relationship. He even asked me to marry him, but I was no longer interested.

Joe's daughter lost the lease on her house and was evicted, according to my divorce attorney. Since I was the leaseholder, I had requested to be off the lease after the assault, which is my right as a victim of domestic violence under the law. My attorney sent the leasing company notice of this situation, and due to Joe's lack of employment, she was evicted. This is not the outcome I would have wanted, but I could not continue to be responsible for Joe's daughter's living expenses. I do not know where she is now, but my prayers and heart go out to her. I cannot imagine what horrors she must have lived through from her father.

And as for Joe, I can only assume he is not in jail but under the probation guidelines set forth by the courts. While he wears an ankle monitor, which should be a red flag to anyone, I have no doubt he is able to smooth talk his way into numerous women's lives as he did mine. I pray for the safety of all who encounter him, as he is a predator and has no regard for human life or the law.

My personal thoughts on Joe? I know that Joe is demon-possessed. I saw his transformation on numerous occasions, but I did not recognize it early on. I believe he is a psychopath and narcissist incapable of anything but control. He did tell me that his wife, who died, would get better and then not need him anymore. As a matter of fact, she would see her previous boyfriend while Joe was married to her. She did not try to hide this from Joe and would blatantly engage in going to see him.

I believe Joe started to poison her so he could control her, but he overdid it and killed her accidentally. He had her body cremated so no one could know his secret. From that moment on, he wanted to relive those last moments of her life with other victims. In his madness and demon possession, he became a serial killer. I am so thankful to God as He intervened so I could escape with my life. I do pray for Joe and have forgiven Him, not for him but for me. I know that one day, Joe will stand in judgment for his heinous acts of violence toward others.

As you can see from many of those involved in my story, the repercussions of domestic violence reach far beyond the one who is being abused or the abuser. The long arms of sin can stretch far beyond the boundaries of the sinner. All sin has consequences, sometimes even to those who are innocent. This is the consequence of living in a fallen world.

MY URGENT MESSAGE

The main purpose of telling my story is to get an urgent message out to those who may be suffering a similar fate. Every day, I see news stories about murder-suicide or a boyfriend killing a girlfriend or vice-versa. There is no need to continue to suffer. Whether you are an abuser or being abused, GET HELP! I am sure you may be thinking how easy it is for me to say this now that I am out of my situation, but I still have moments of doubt. Not of doubt that I should have left the relationship but doubt if I am free and never have to worry about Joe coming back to take revenge on me. He is still out there and could easily find me if he wanted to do this. Although I have found comfort in the message provided by the federal marshals on his arrest, I still struggle at times with fear. But as much fear as I have, I have that much more faith. I have faith that I will be protected by God's angel armies and that in obeying His commandment to tell my story, I will be protected as I get His Word out.

I know there are several times in my story you may have thought in your reading, why did you not just leave? I have asked myself that many times, and I do not have a satisfactory answer. All I can say is that I was under the manipulation of a psychopath. I wish I had recognized this much earlier and never had to write this book, but that is not what happened. No one counseled me on how to behave in these situations, and I was naïve. I never imagined I would encounter demons or evil such as this, as I was weak. It was only through Christ that I was strong enough to survive it and make it out.

"I can do all things through him who strengthens me."

PHILIPPIANS 4:13 ESV

I know, based on the statistics, there are many in danger or suffering because of domestic abuse and do not know they have the strength to leave or endure, as they have been repeatedly manipulated or broken down in spirit. This is the main reason my message is so urgent to those who may be in danger of this type of manipulation.

"I can't impress this on you too strongly. God is looking over your shoulder. Christ himself is the Judge, with the final say on everyone, living and dead. He is about to break into the open with his rule, so proclaim the Message with intensity; keep on your watch. Challenge, warn, and urge your people. Don't ever quit. Just keep it simple."

2 TIMOTHY 4:1-2

Remember these seven truths about domestic violence:

1) There is no demographic, age, ethnic, gender, or racial barriers or boundaries for domestic violence. It is an equal opportunity offender.

2) Know the warning signs (or red flags) of behavior that may be a precursor to domestic violence. Get out early in the relationship once you see the signs, do not look back, and get help.

3) Do not buy into the lies of the enemy—especially, if they tell you that marriage or other commitments will make the situation better.

4) Jesus is calling us into freedom. He is calling us into a new life, free from the guilt and shame of abuse.

5) People and relationships can be toxic and evil, even if those involved are believers. We are not required to be around toxic or abusive people, even if they are family members.

6) God SEES YOU right in your circumstances and has a plan for your life.

7) There is healing and life after domestic violence.

It is time to step into a new season of life, free from abuse! Blessings to you all.

Hope Elizabeth Powers

While my story may not be typical, if you are suffering abuse of any kind, get help. Do not wait until it is too late, and your story is broadcast on the nightly news.

National Domestic Violence Hotline
800-799-7233

ABOUT THE AUTHOR

Hope Elizabeth Powers holds a Bachelor of Science degree from a Christian University, as well as a master's degree and an MBA. With a background in the sciences, Hope has published numerous articles in academic journals, as well as a variety of articles for local publications. During the day, she works in full-time ministry and is a writer by night. When she isn't working or writing, she enjoys spending time with her children, grandchildren, and dogs.

Hope shares her harrowing experience of survival and how God moved in a redemptive way to rescue her in her first book, *Journey to the Beginning, Escaping Domestic Violence and Living to Tell My Story*. In telling her story, she provides a message of hope to those who are enduring or have endured domestic violence or abuse. The message that Jesus has called us into freedom from the guilt and shame of abuse is Hope's passionate message that she weaves throughout her story.

HopePowers.com

ENDNOTES

1   "NCADV: National Coalition Against Domestic Violence." *The Nation's Leading Grassroots Voice on Domestic Violence*, https:// www.ncadv.org/statistics.

2   *Cinderella Syndrome "Women with Fear of ... - Researchgate.* https://www.researchgate.net/publication/348910838_ Cinderella_Syndrome_Women_with_Fear_of_Independence_ Developing_a_Scale.

3   "Aftershock Definition & Meaning." *Merriam-Webster*, Merriam- Webster, https://www.merriam-webster.com/dictionary/ aftershock.

4   Foreman, John. *Https://Switchfoot.com/Blogs/News/Stories-behind- the-Songs-Live-It-Well.*

5   "Crusader." *CRUSADER | Definition in the Cambridge English Dictionary*, https://dictionary.cambridge.org/us/dictionary/ english/crusader.

6   "Crusade." *The Free Dictionary*, Farlex, https://www. thefreedictionary.com/crusade.

Made in the USA
Coppell, TX
04 February 2023

12126239R00118